© Copyright 2012 Lloyd Mathews BSc (Hons)

About the author: I have a Bachelor of Science degree in aquaculture and a Bachelor of Science (with Honours) in environmental biology. Recently, I spent several years running my own fishpond maintenance business. I am currently building a small goldfish hatchery and a small aquaponics set-up on my home property. I also teach science, part-time, in high schools.

Important note: If you are looking for information about a particular thing, and you can't find it in the "Contents" pages, try looking in the **glossary** at the end of the book. Many of the terms in the glossary have references to more information in the book.

Introduction

My aim in this book is to give essential advice on all the main aspects of freshwater garden fish ponds. I have tried to include some of the science of ponds while keeping the information easy to understand. Each chapter begins with an outline of the main points of the topic. Each point is then expanded on.

My experience with ponds has mainly been in the warm temperate of climate in Perth, Western Australia. The principles for fish ponds are similar worldwide but warm temperate climates like that of Perth intensify some of the problems in ponds. This book will therefore be particularly useful to pond owners in sunny climates.

The book begins with **pond design**, starting with the **position** of the pond in the garden. I discuss the consequences of different **pond sizes and depths** and of **"natural"** and **"artificial"** ponds. I talk about the advantages of a **dual pond system**. I give guidelines for these and for **"self-cleaning" ponds**. I also say why I recommend designing the pond with a **sump, overflow, leaf skimmer,** and **automatic top-up valve**. Lastly, I give my **colour** preference for the pond bottom and sides.

Next, I advise on **pond construction**. Ponds can be built with **concrete, bricks, rigid polyethylene, fibreglass** or **liners**. I write about my experiences with ponds made from each of these materials and also my preferences for **pipework** materials.

In the following chapter, I recommend various **pumps, filters** (including **ultraviolet clarifiers**), **water features, underwater lights** and **copper ionizers**. Choosing the right equipment will give you the right effect for the lowest cost and for the least effort.

The chapter on fish gives information on types of fish, especially **goldfish** and **koi**. I advise on **when a new pond is ready for fish** and the **number of fish** a pond can support. I give information on the **handling, transporting,** and **feeding of fish**, and on **diseases** and **predators**.

The next chapter delivers general information on **water plants** – why you should have them and their role in the ecology of the pond. Plants provide shade, oxygen, food, habitat and cover from predators. They **filter toxins and excessive nutrients** from the water. I give advice on keeping plants, including information on **fertilizer and pests**.

Finally, I give recommendations for **pond maintenance** including a routine. My advice is directed at **pumps, filters,** pond **cleanliness, exchanging water** and maintaining the **pH and hardness**. The maintenance is largely directed at **algae control**. I discuss the various forms of nuisance algae and control methods control for microalgae, blanket weed, and slime algae. Other advice includes information on **water testing** and **water treatments**.

Maintaining good **water quality** is fundamental to the success of any fish pond. "Good" water quality means the water's suitability for its proposed purpose. Water quality is affected by every aspect of a pond, from its design and construction to its pumps, filters and maintenance. Each chapter of this book tells how each aspect of the pond affects the water. Every fish pond is different. The solutions to one pond's problems may be very different to another pond's.

Contents

Chapter 1: Design

The main design considerations for a pond	8
Position	9
Size and depth	12
Natural or artificial	15
Two connected ponds - an ideal set-up	20
Self-cleaning ponds	22
Sumps	23
Overflow	24
Leaf skimmer	24
Automatic water top-up	25
Colour	25
Construction materials	25
Water features	26

Chapter 2: Construction

The most common materials used	27
Concrete	28
Rendered brick	30
Polyethylene	32
Fibreglass	33
Liners of rubber and plastic	34
Pipes of PVC, polyethylene and vinyl	36

Chapter 3: Pond Equipment

The main items of equipment	38
Pumps	39
Filters – mechanical, biological, UV clarifier	47
Leaf skimmer	55
Water features	55
Underwater lights	63
Copper ionizer	63

Chapter 4: Fish

The main considerations for pond fish…	65
Do you need fish?	66
How many fish?	66
What kind of fish?	69
When do you put the fish in?	71
Handling fish	73
Transporting fish	74
Feeding fish	78
Fish diseases	81
Fish predators	92
Goldfish	93
Koi	97

Chapter 5: Water Plants

The main considerations for water plants	99
Plants shade the water	100
Filtration of nutrients and toxic contaminants	101
Keep plants in pots	104
Don't fertilize	105
Dissolved oxygen	105
Food, habitat, and cover from predators	106
Pests	107
Types of plants	107

Chapter 6: Maintenance

The main considerations for maintenance	**111**
Maintain pumps	**112**
Keep filters clean	**113**
Don't overfeed the fish	**116**
Keep the pond clean and exchange water	**117**
Maintain the pH and hardness	**124**
Control algae	**126**
Pond treatments	**136**
Have a maintenance routine	**138**

Glossary   141

Chapter 1
Design

The main design considerations for a pond are:

- *Position*
- *Size and depth*
- *Natural or artificial?*
- *Two connected ponds – an ideal set-up*
- *Self-cleaning ponds*
- *Sumps*
- *Overflow*
- *Leaf skimmer*
- *Automatic water top-up*
- *Colour*
- *Construction materials*
- *Water features*

Position

The main considerations for the position of ponds are:

♦ ***Sunlight:*** Too much sunlight will grow excessive algae.

♦ ***Trees:*** One of the main sources of nutrients for algae is leaves.

♦ ***Proximity to the property boundary:*** Chemical sprays and leaves can drift in from the neighbours' properties. Noise from falling water and frogs might annoy the neighbours.

This pond is in the shade and away from trees and the property's boundaries. The water and fountain have no bad algae problems, even in warm weather.

♦ Sunlight

The main point when positioning a pond is the **amount of sunlight** it will get. In very cold climates, you might need the pond to be in the sun for most of the day. I am told that in Germany ponds need six to eight hours of sunlight a day, but in the south of England a few hours a day is enough. However, in winter the ponds probably need all the sunlight they can get, but in the middle of summer they probably need very little direct sunlight. Often the solution is to position the pond to have sunlight in the winter and shade in the summer.

In warm or hot climates, during the warm seasons, ponds should be in the shade all of the time. Sunlight provides the energy for algae growth. Shade is the key to controlling algae. I have seen ponds side by side with the ones in the shade all day looking great and the others in the sun most of the time continually looking a mess of unsightly algae.

To shade a pond in a warm climate, put a structure such as a **shaded pergola** over it or build the pond **under the eaves of the shadiest side of the house**. You could make a framework over which you fix shadecloth in summer and clear plastic in winter, or use a moveable structure. **Water plants** also provide shade.

♦ Trees

The shade should not be provided by trees. All trees shed leaves. Some lose them all at once, in autumn, while others lose them slowly throughout the year. Bacteria decompose leaves in the bottom of ponds releasing nutrients and noxious contaminants into the water. The bacteria also consume large quantities of oxygen.

♦ Proximity to the property boundary

The pond should also be **away from the property's boundary** reducing the danger of **chemical sprays** (pesticides and so on) and **leaves** drifting in from neighbouring properties. Also, the soothing **sound of running water** irritates some people so the further the pond is from the boundary the less the chance of neighbourly warfare.

This fountain is in direct sunlight for most of the day. It is too far from the trees to benefit from their shade during the hottest part of the day but it is close enough for the wind to continually dump leaves into the water. The only good point about its position is that it is placed as far from the property boundaries as possible.

Size and depth

The main considerations for the size and depth of ponds are:

◆ *The safety of children:* If the pond is too deep, it will need to be in a fenced yard or to be covered with safety mesh. You will need to check your local government regulations.

◆ *Environmental stability:* The larger and deeper the pond, the more stable the temperature and other factors affecting water quality.

◆ *The safety of children*

The safest depth for toddlers is no more than **25 centimetres (10 inches)** at the edge of the pond with only a very gradual slope to deeper water (pond bottoms are slippery). If the pond is raised above ground level, toddlers will be less likely to accidentally fall in.

Ponds deeper than 25 centimetres near the edge should be either in a fenced yard or covered with **safety mesh** strong enough to support the weight of a child. For ponds with plants or fish, the mesh should be made of nylon, strong plastic, or **stainless steel**.

Galvanized or mild steel mesh will add toxic zinc or iron to the water when it rains (even unpolluted rain water is slightly acidic). The mesh should be fixed in a way that stops children removing it but allows you to take it off to clean the pond.

This pond is in a fenced yard and although it is half a metre deep, it is fully raised above the ground and has a clean, flat bottom. If toddlers are capable of climbing into the pond, they should be capable of standing up and getting out (or screaming for you to help them). Remember though, toddlers are completely safe only when you are watching them.

♦ *Environmental stability*

The larger the pond, the more it looks after itself. Large ponds are more environmentally stable and offer greater variety of habitat than small ponds so it is more likely that nature will keep them healthy. Ideally, a pond should be at least a hundred square metres in area and over a metre deep.

Realistically, if your pond is **at least two square metres in area** (about two square yards**) and half a metre deep** (approximately one and a half feet), it shouldn't be too difficult to look after. With ponds over half a metre deep, built-in ledges are handy for some types of plants.

The water in large, deep ponds with no pump can become **stratified** - a stagnant layer of water forms on the bottom of the pond. In temperate climates this probably won't happen in ponds less than two metres deep. As the surface water cools at night, it sinks to the bottom of the pond pushing the bottom water upwards to the surface. By coming into contact with air, the water takes up oxygen and releases undesirable gases such as carbon dioxide.

For some species of **fish**, for example koi, the water should ideally be at least a metre (a yard) deep. Koi like to dive. They can injure themselves on the bottom of shallow ponds. I have seen wounds on large koi in shallow ponds.

For a fish to be healthy, the **temperature** needs to remain within the fish's tolerance limits. For example, with goldfish the lower limit is 4 degrees centigrade (about 40 degrees Fahrenheit) and the upper limit is about 30 degrees centigrade (about 85 degrees Fahrenheit).

Pond size and depth help control temperature. For instance, in cold climates the pond needs to be large enough and deep enough so that the water at the bottom doesn't freeze in winter. In warm and hot climates, goldfish ponds need to be large enough and deep enough to prevent the temperature from reaching 30 degrees centigrade at the bottom.

Also, **swings in temperature** are very stressful for fish. The larger and deeper the pond, the more stable the temperature will be. The temperature of water changes more slowly than the temperature of the surrounding air because the air is moving. The surrounding air is constantly being replaced by other air so its temperature range is a lot more than the pond's range.

As a general guide, the minimum depth I recommend for cold and hot climates is one metre. For warm climates, the minimum depth I would want is half a metre (more if the pond is in the sun for much of the day).

Natural or artificial?

The two extreme types of ponds are:

♦ *Natural ponds:* The **larger** the better and the more **plants** the better.

♦ *Artificial ponds:* Design the pond to be as easy to clean as possible and use all available technology.

Of course, a pond can be anywhere between a natural pond and an artificial pond. A truly natural pond is a lake which might have underground or surface water flowing through it. An example of a truly artificial pond is a chlorinated water feature devoid of fish or plants.

♦ *Natural ponds*

Healthy natural ponds in the wild usually have water flow-through. Even ponds that seem to be stagnant generally have some underground flow. Toxic substances are constantly being taken away with the flowing water.

In a warm climate, to have your pond as a natural ecosystem which will never need cleaning, make it **at least a hundred square metres in area** with an average **depth of at least a metre**. I would have a layer of **sand** about 100 millimetres deep on the bottom. The sand would be a habitat for anaerobic bacteria which would break down nitrates. I would cover the sand with a 100 millimetre (4 inch) layer of **gravel**. The gravel layer would act as a habitat for nitrifying bacteria which convert toxic ammonia and nitrites to less toxic nitrates. The gravel would also provide aerated anchorage for water plants because water can flow through the gravel.

Some **aeration** occurs at the surface of ponds where the water contacts the air above it, especially when the water and air are moving past each other. Providing the water isn't too deep, every night as the surface water cools it sinks displacing the water below it. Oxygen from the air is carried down with the water as it sinks. The maximum depth to which this nightly turnover operate depend on the local climate. It could be anywhere between 1 metre and 4 metres (approximately 3 feet and 12 feet).

Ideally, have a large **pump** sending the water 24 hours a day through a fountain or waterfall to help aerate the water. Draw the water from a network of slotted pipes buried under the gravel so that the gravel filters solid particles from the water and flow occurs in all parts of the pond. The perfect pump would be large enough to turn over the volume of the pond every two hours but any pump will help to aerate the water.

The main reason for having **water plants** is to take up nutrients, especially phosphorus that would otherwise be available to produce algae. Using plants for aeration doesn't really work because plants use oxygen at night but don't produce any. The most important time to have your pump running, therefore, is during the early hours of the morning, just before sunrise.

Design the pond with **raised banks** to prevent water running in from the surrounding land bringing fertilizer, leaves, pesticides and other rubbish into the pond. Slope the banks gradually into the water to make it safer for children and to encourage plants that grow partly out of the water. These plants are called emergents.

Plant much of the bottom immediately with emergent plants of all kinds. The deepest parts of the pond should be planted first. The pond should only be partly filled – just enough to cover the plants. The water level should be raised as the plants grow. Plant the higher banks as the water covers them. Allow the emergents to rise above the surface of the water before introducing floating plants. If the emergents are shaded by floating plants, they will die adding nutrients to the water which will encourage algae to establish.

Cover much of the surface with floating plants. I wouldn't plant submergent plants (these plants live entirely under water). As floating plants and emergents die, you can remove them before they rot and pollute the water with nutrients. You can't easily see when submergents die.

The sooner plants establish, the sooner they take up nutrients from the water that would otherwise encourage algae to establish. Plants also secrete chemicals which inhibit algae. If plants are quickly established in a new pond, it makes it harder for algae to get started. To keep the pH around neutral I would add agricultural lime or an acid – whichever is needed (see *Maintain the pH and hardness* on page 124). Add no fertilizer whatsoever.

The pond above has elements of a natural pond: vegetation and a pebble-covered bottom. It has good water flow and aeration delivered by a large pump which sends the water over a waterfall. The water is drawn into the pump through perforated pipes under the pebbles. However, the pond is too shallow and is in the sun for most of the day. Ugly, scum-like algae build up quickly on the bottom making it necessary to vacuum it every few weeks.

The photo below, taken a few years ago, shows a large pond on my home property which has underground water flowing through it. The water quality was very good – it has only a slight green algae bloom. Fifteen years ago, the water was almost totally clear.

The next photo, taken at the end of last summer, is of the same pond as the one above. The water quality has greatly deteriorated and it has a reddish-brown algae bloom. What happened? The main cause of the problem is decreased underground water flow because of lower rainfall. The field above the pond is a favourite grazing place for kangaroos. Their faeces and plant matter (grass and tree leaves) are being washed into the pond where they break down and add dissolved nutrients to the water. Also, trees have grown close to the pond's edge and are now continually shedding leaves into the water. Because the underground flow is no longer fast enough to carry the nutrients away quickly, an explosion in algae growth has occurred.

How do I fix this? Apart from praying to the Gods to get rid of the Greenhouse Effect, I need to dig a drain around the high side of the pond and to cut down all the trees growing close to the water.

♦ *Artificial ponds*

For artificial ponds, direct all aspects of design towards maintaining good water quality with minimum effort. That means designing the pond to be as easy to clean as possible and to use all available pond technology. For ease of maintenance, have a **bare bottom** (the pond, not you). Have **no sand, gravel or pebbles** whatsoever on the bottom of the pond. Sand, gravel and pebbles make cleaning very difficult. **Keep all plants in pots** so that they can be easily removed when the pond is cleaned.

Pump the water through **mechanical and biological filters.** The pump should be large enough to circulate all the water every two hours. If microscopic algae in suspension become so dense that you can't see the fish on the bottom of the pond, install an **ultraviolet clarifier**. If leaves are a nuisance, put in a **leaf skimmer**. For more information on pond technology, see *Chapter 3: Pond Equipment* on page 38. Toxic substances can accumulate with time so some **water exchange** will be necessary.

Two connected ponds - an ideal set-up

Two connected ponds, with one as a *plant filter pond* is an ideal set-up.

One main advantage of having two connected ponds is the **ease of maintenance**. Most small ponds need cleaning at least once a year. When you clean a pond you remove all the natural biological systems that have developed. If you have two connected ponds, clean one pond at a time and wait a few months before cleaning the other. Nature's healthy balance will be re-established quickly in the cleaned pond through the transfer of organisms from the second pond.

To save pumping costs and increase aeration, the ponds should be set up so that one feeds by gravity into the other through, for example, a waterfall.

Another major advantage of two ponds is that one of them can be filled with plants to filter nitrates and phosphates from the water while the other pond can be kept clear for observing fish such as koi. The **plant pond** could be run as a natural pond with a layer of gravel on the bottom. The **fish pond** can be easily cleaned when necessary while the plant pond can be flushed clean once every two or three years. It takes a lot of plants to filter the wastes from a few fish. If you have a lot of fish, the plant filter pond should be larger than the fish pond or the plants should be thick and tall.

If you have two ponds connected by the water from one flowing by gravity into the other, all the water loss due to evaporation will lower the water level only in the lower pond. If the lower pond is much smaller than the upper pond, the level in the lower pond can drop quickly on days with hot, dry winds. If the smaller pond is below the larger pond, it is important to have an automatic water top-up valve in the lower pond to maintain the water level. Otherwise, the best design is with the larger pond below the smaller one. In that case, the plant pond will be below the fish pond. Self-cleaning ponds are opposite - the fish pond will normally be below the plant pond because a powerful pump is needed in the fish pond to remove the wastes (see *An ideal pond* on page 26).

This photo shows a small plant pond above a larger, deeper koi pond. Although the plant pond is small, the plants are mainly "elephant ears" which grow huge and so remove large amounts of nitrates and phosphates from the water. The drawback with elephant ears is that they are toxic to fish if they eat them.

Self-cleaning ponds

The main considerations for self-cleaning ponds are:

- ◆ ***Pond shape: Circular or oval ponds*** that have no major obstructions to interfere with circular flow can be self-cleaning.
- ◆ ***Diameter to depth ratio of the pond:*** should ideally be close to 3:1 (for example, three metres in diameter to one metre in depth).

◆ *Pond shape*

Yes, there is such a thing as a self-cleaning pond. The problem is that the pond has to be **circular or oval** and have no major obstructions to interfere with circular flow. Also, unless you have a leaf skimmer or no leaves at all falling into the pond, you will need a pump capable of handling leaves.

The water is sent into the pond at an angle to cause a **circular flow** so that sediments on the bottom of the pond gravitate towards the centre. From the centre, the water is drawn off by a pump then sent through a filter before being returned to the pond.

It isn't necessary to have an outlet cut through the bottom of the pond for the pump to draw the water out of the pond. As long as the mouth of the pump's suction pipe is close to the bottom and the pump is powerful enough, it will suck up the sediments.

The circular shape of the pond can be broken up with overhanging features, plants and so on which are clear of the water. The bottom of the pond can be flat, but if the bottom slopes down to the centre, it helps the movement of sediment to the centre.

◆ *Diameter to depth ratio*

For self-cleaning to happen in flat-bottomed ponds, **the diameter to depth ratio has to be less than 4.5 to1 and ideally should be 3 to 1** (for example, three metres in diameter and one metre deep). Also, if the bottom is flat, the water flow velocity should be at least 15 centimetres (6 inches) per second.

For the health of most fish species, the maximum flow velocity is two fish body lengths per second which means that self-cleaning ponds with a flat bottom are practical only for fish longer than 7.5 centimetres (three inches). For smaller fish, the pond bottom will have to slope to the centre so that the water flow velocity can be decreased but the sediments will still move towards the centre.

Sumps

Unless the pond is self-cleaning, to make cleaning easier the pond should have a sump – a small area deeper than the rest of the pond. The last of the water and sludge can be pumped from the sump. Ideally, the pond bottom should slope slightly downwards to the sump. All the mud and debris on the bottom of the pond can be hosed into the sump and, except for large pieces of rubbish, pumped or drained out. Of the hundreds of ponds I've cleaned, very few had a sump and most of them had a flat bottom. Mopping or vacuuming up the muck and the last of the water was very time-consuming.

If your pond is raised and can be gravity drained, you can have a drain hole at the lowest point in the sump. The pond can then be drained without using a pump. Drain holes are a potential source of leaks, however, and drain lines are prone to blocking up. Make the **drain line at least 15 centimetres (6 inches) in diameter with no bends more than 45 degrees.** Put a suitable **strainer over the drain hole.**

Overflow

A screened overflow pipe is necessary to prevent overflowing pond water taking your fish for a swim in the garden. If you live in an area of high rainfall or sudden storms, a screened overflow is a must. Otherwise, your fish might one day be liberated into the garden. The overflow pipe should be **at least 5 centimetres (2 inches) in diameter** and the overflow **screen** should be as coarse as possible. It should keep your fish in but not block up too easily. Ideally, put a very coarse screen on the end of the overflow pipe inside of the pond and a finer screen on the outside end to prevent the fish escaping. Slope the pipe downwards back into the pond so fish won't be stranded in the pipe.

Leaf Skimmer

Leaf skimmers are ideal for removing *leaves* from ponds. They consist of a pump drawing water from the surface of the pond through a basket which catches the leaves.

The main cause of displeasure with ponds is excessive algae. Algae need nutrients to grow. **The main source of nutrients for most ponds is leaves**. Even if you keep trees away from the pond, the wind might bring leaves there. Unless you have the time to scoop out the leaves every day before they sink, include a leaf skimmer in the pond design.

By far the best skimmers are set into the side of the pond. It is much easier to incorporate them into the pond when it is constructed than to add them later because you would have to cut into the side of the pond.

You should empty the leaves from the basket before they begin decomposing, adding nutrients to the water. Stand-alone skimmers can be set up anywhere in the pond. They usually have very small baskets to catch the leaves, so you need to empty them often.

Automatic water top-up

In regions which have seasons with **high evaporation**, an automatic top-up valve will save time and worry. You still need to check the pond's water level occasionally to see that the valve is working but a glance at is all it takes. Install the most reliable valve available. They are cheap, but bringing the plumbing to the pond may be costly unless you have a suitable garden reticulation line passing close by.

If you are taking the water from the town water supply you might need to install a **non-return valve** that meets the local water authority's specifications. One way around this is to have the opening of the top-up valve above the top of the pond walls. Unless you have bizarre tastes (like my dogs) you don't want fishpond water moving back into your drinking water supply.

If you have a reticulation system which operates via an automatic timer, a cheap but inaccurate top up method is to drop one of the reticulation sprinklers into the pond. Then, every time you water the garden, you top up the pond.

Colour

For the walls and bottom of the pond, ***black*** is the best colour. The background colour of a pond will affect the pond's appearance. White ponds, like white shirts, show dirt, and there is always dirt in a pond. Even though pond surfaces become coated with algae and other organisms, dark-coloured ponds always look cleaner than light-coloured ponds. Also, the colours of most fish show up better against a dark background.

Construction materials

When designing a pond, consider which materials you want to use because the materials influence the design. For more information about materials, refer to *Chapter 2*, page 27.

Water features

Water features will affect the pond design. A waterfall or leaf skimmer might be built into the pond wall. A heavy fountain will need a solid pond bottom on which to stand. For more information, refer to *Water features* on page 55.

An ideal pond

```
        ┌─────────────┐
   ┌───▶│ FILTER :    │
   │    │ Mechanical, │
   │    │ biological  │
   │    │ and UV      │
   │    └─────────────┘
   │           │
   │           ▼
   │    ┌──────────────────────────┐
   │    │  PLANT POND              │
   │    │   🍁        🍁           │
   │    └──────────────────────────┘
   │              │
   │          CASCADE
   │              ▼
   │    ╭──────────────────────╮
   │    │  FISH POND           │
   │    │  (self-cleaning)     │──⊗
   │    │                      │   │
   │    │   Pump in sump       │   │
   │    ╰──────────────────────╯   │
   │         │                     │
   └─────────┘                     │
                                   │
          OVERFLOW ⇩       ONE-WAY VALVE
                           TO AUTOMATIC
                           TOP-UP VALVE
```

Chapter 2
Construction

The most common materials used are:

- *Concrete*
- *Rendered brick*
- *Polyethylene*
- *Fibreglass*
- *Liners of rubber and plastic*
- *Pipes of PVC, polyethylene & vinyl*

Concrete

The main considerations for building concrete ponds are:

- ♦ ***Thickness:*** Preferably 150 millimetres (6 inches) but can be less.
- ♦ ***Reinforcing:*** Use galvanized steel mesh.
- ♦ ***Pouring:*** Pour the concrete quickly and in one go. Use a vibrator.
- ♦ ***Dual ponds:*** If building dual concrete ponds, connect them with flexible material.
- ♦ ***Sealing:*** The concrete should be painted with a sealant. Prevent moisture entering between the concrete and sealant by placing a sheet of plastic on the ground before pouring the concrete.

♦ *Thickness*

For cold countries, the concrete needs to be **150mm (six inches) thick** or it could crack in the winter freeze. In warm climates, the concrete shouldn't be less than 100mm (four inches) for small ponds and 150mm for large ponds.

♦ *Reinforcing*

Reinforce the concrete with galvanized steel mesh. If ordinary mild steel mesh is used, and water seeps into the concrete from the pond, the steel will rust and eventually rupture the concrete. I heard a story about a farmer whose tank had "exploded". At first, he believed the neighbour's boys had blown it up. Although the tank was only twelve years old, the concrete had suddenly given way under the pressure of the steel expanding with rust. Galvanized chicken mesh has been used to build concrete boats including yachts because it is easy to shape and the cement can be sprayed onto the mesh. I can't see why it wouldn't be suitable for building ponds.

♦ Pouring

The **concrete for the whole pond should be poured as quickly as possible**. Concrete binds much better when it is wet – don't stop for lunch in the middle of pouring. If you do, you may leave a line of weakness which could crack. Use a **concrete vibrator** to expel all air from the concrete making it stronger.

♦ Dual ponds

If you build two joined concrete ponds, pour them as one solid unit (joined across the full width of the ponds). If you do them separately, link them with some sort of flexible material. I have seen two concrete ponds joined by a narrow concrete canal. The whole thing was built as a single unit. In time, the ground sank a little beneath the ponds, as it invariably does with the huge weight of the concrete and water pushing down. Ground often doesn't sink uniformly. One of the ponds sank at a different rate to the other causing the canal and adjoining parts of the ponds to rupture.

♦ Sealing

To extend the life of the pond, paint the walls and floor with a **sealant** after the concrete is dry. Use only products recommended for permanent immersion in water and which are guaranteed to be **non-toxic**. Do the job well - even a pin-hole opening in the sealant will allow moisture to get behind it possibly lifting it off the concrete. Also, **record the name and specifications of the sealant.** If you have to touch up the paint years later, you could have disastrous results if the new sealant isn't compatible with the old sealant. To be certain that moisture can't penetrate from below the concrete and lift off the sealant, place a **liner of builder's plastic** on the ground before pouring the concrete.

An alternative to painting is rendering with mortar containing a non-toxic **water-proofing additive** in place of lime. See the information on water-proofing on the next page.

The concrete pond above was incorporated into the brick boundary wall (the wall is on a street corner, away from neighbours).

Rendered brick

The main considerations for building ponds in brick are:

♦ ***Concrete base / brick walls:*** The bottom of the pond is done in concrete to support the walls which can be single brick, double brick or cement blocks. The inside walls of the pond are then rendered with mortar and water-proofed.

♦ ***Water-proofing:*** *Using* one of the following procedures:
1. Mix an additive in with the render.
2. Paint the dried render with a sealant.
3. Apply a two-coat epoxy resin to the render.
4. Fibreglass the inside of the pond.
5. Insert a liner.
6. Build the pond around a preformed fibreglass or polyethylene shell.

◆ *Concrete base / brick walls*

The **base of the pond is poured in concrete** (see the previous section on concrete). Make the concrete base thicker around the edges where the walls are to be supported and use extra galvanized steel mesh reinforcing along the edges. Providing the pond is not more than half a metre (one and a half feet) deep, it can be built with **single brick walls**. If most of the pond is below ground level, single brick will be all right for up to three quarters of a metre (two and a half feet). For deeper ponds, the walls should be of **double brick with steel ties**. Hollow **cement blocks** can also be used and preferably filled afterwards with concrete.

I wouldn't cement rocks together to make walls because in time cracks usually appear where the mortar joins the rocks resulting in leaks. This probably happens because the mortar expands and contracts with heat and cold at a different rate to the rocks. I would reserve rocks and stone for decorative purposes only.

◆ *Water-proofing procedures*

1. Render the brick walls with a cement mix which includes a non-toxic **water-proofing additive** in place of lime.

2. Paint the pond render with a sealant. **Don't try to paint a sealant over cement render which contains a water-proofing additive** because the sealant probably won't stick properly. In time, the sealant will peel away from the render leaving a mess. If using a **paint-on sealant**, even a **pin-hole opening in the sealant will allow moisture to get behind it** lifting it off the render.

Also, if the concrete bottom is painted with sealant, lay a **liner of builder's plastic** on the ground before pouring the concrete. The plastic will prevent moisture penetrating the concrete. I have seen ponds where moisture has caused the sealant to bubble away from the pond walls eventually rupturing causing leaks. When this happens, the only solution is to insert a liner.

There is a range of water-based and oil-based paint-on sealants. **Keep a record of the sealant you use!** Then when you need to touch up or re-coat the sealant, you can use exactly the same product again. Mixing different types of sealant can be disastrous.

The cheapest paint-on sealant is **bitumen paint**. It sticks well to the concrete giving a good seal and it is non-toxic to fish. Read the paint's instructions - a second type of sealant is usually needed to prevent sunlight damage. Like some of the more expensive sealants, it stays soft underneath the surface so that narrow cracks don't break the seal. Because it is soft underneath, however, it is easily scratched.

3. Another alternative is to use a **two-coat epoxy resin**. The resin often doesn't stick well to the pond walls, but it forms a very tough shell.

4. The best coating to use on concrete or cement render is **fibreglass**, but it is also the most expensive.

5. A **liner** of PVC, polyethylene, polypropylene or butyl rubber can be made to fit into the pond (see the section on page 32 on *Liners*).

6. The pond can be built around a **preformed fibreglass or polyethylene** shell. In my opinion, this is the best method. You may not find a preformed shell of the size and shape you want, however.

Polyethylene

Preformed thick polyethylene ("plastic") ponds come in all shapes and sizes and last for decades. All you need to do is dig a hole to put it in or build a decorative wall of stone, brick or some other material around it. They are more expensive than preformed fibreglass.

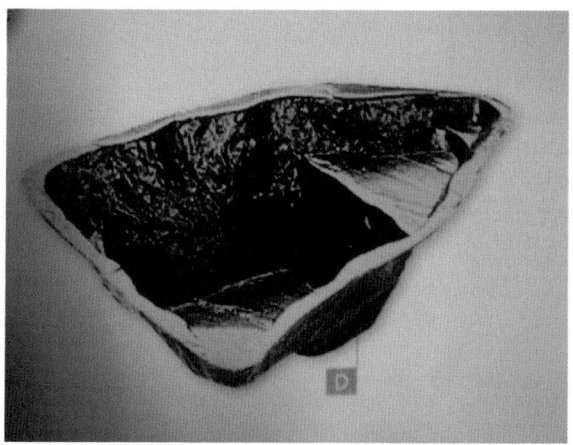

A pre-formed polyethylene pond. *Photo courtesy of Aquatec Equipment, Maddington, Western Australia.*

Fibreglass

Fibreglass ponds can be:

- ♦ ***pre-formed in a mould.*** As long as they have a proper finishing layer applied to prevent damage by sunlight, they will last for many years.
- ♦ ***custom-made.*** Fibreglass ponds come in a range of shapes and sizes. If you can't find one that is suitable, you can have one custom made. They are, however, much more expensive than pre-formed ponds.
- ♦ ***constructed of other materials*** (concrete, brick, stone, marine plywood etc.) and then fibreglassed.
- ♦ ***harmful to fish.*** Some fish fanciers are not happy with fibreglass because the fish can be injured by fibres if they brush against a damaged part of the wall. Some pond people still prefer fibreglass to polyethylene, however, because they can move the pond without damaging it. Polyethylene does eventually become slightly brittle with exposure to sunlight.

Liners of rubber and plastic

A liner is a sheet of any waterproof material used to line a pond.

The main considerations for building a liner pond are:

♦ ***Below ground:*** Dig a hole with raised edges.

♦ ***Above ground:*** Build walls with concrete, brick, stone or marine plywood and insert a liner.

♦ ***Types of liners:*** "Builder's plastic", polyethylene, PVC, polypropylene, butyl rubber.

♦ ***Below ground***

Liners are the cheapest way to build a pond. All you need to do is dig a hole in the ground. **Build up a mound 15 centimetres (6 inches) high and at least half a metre (one and a half feet) wide around the pond to prevent run-off entering the pond.**

If the ground isn't sand, then cover the whole excavation including the surrounding mound with 15 centimetres (6 inches) of sand to cushion the liner when you walk in the pond.

Spread the liner in the hole and overlap the mound around the hole. Cover the edges of the liner with decorative stones to keep it in place. The walls of the pond need to be sloping at least 45 degrees or the walls might collapse.

♦ Above ground

If you want an above-ground pond, concrete and brick ponds can be waterproofed by using a liner instead of a concrete additive or a paint-on liner. Materials other than concrete or brick, such as stone or marine plywood, can be used to support a liner.

It isn't essential to concrete the pond bottom, but the pond walls will be more stable if placed on a concrete base. Also, the concrete will give the liner support, protecting it from the weight of people walking in the pond and from heavy water features placed in the pond.

♦ Types of liners

Liner material varies from cheap builder's plastic (very thin polyethylene) to butyl rubber. The life span of a liner depends to a large degree on the amount of exposure to **sunlight** and the strength of the sunlight. For example, in warm climates, where the summer sunlight has strong ultra-violet rays, the life of a liner would be greatly extended if the pond is always in the shade. Also, the **thicker** the liner, the longer it will last. Before buying a liner, always check that the liner material is harmless to fish and plants.

Types of liners include:

1. **Builder's plastic:** This is actually very thin **polyethylene** sheet. I don't recommend this material because it is easily damaged. If you use the thickest grade of builder's plastic (0.2 millimetres) it might last five years. Cover the plastic so none of it is exposed to the sun and don't put any sharp objects in the pond.

   I have worked in ponds that were made by plastering a layer of builder's plastic with mortar. It seems to me to be the worst possible way to build a pond. Unless the mortar is thick enough to allow people to walk on it and unless it is made with a water-proofing additive, I can't see how it can last.

I have cleaned a pond where the mortar had broken down and washed away exposing the plastic. The main reason the mortar failed was because it probably contained lime instead of a water-proofing additive.

2. **Polyethylene liners:** Thick, UV stabilized polyethylene liners will last for more than ten years if the pond is always in the shade.

3. **PVC liners:** PVC, another type of plastic, can be as cheap as polyethylene and often has a lifetime guarantee.

4. **Polypropylene liners:** Polypropylene is another type of plastic. These liners are long-lasting, but are more expensive than PVC and are difficult to fit to the shape of the pond.

5. **Butyl rubber liners:** These are much more expensive than PVC but are much stronger and really do last a lifetime.

Pipes of PVC, polyethylene and vinyl

All these pipes are made of different types of plastic. The main considerations for pond pipes are:

♦ *Outside the pond:* Use PVC or cheap polyethylene hose.

♦ *Inside the pond:* Use black food-grade vinyl hose and black ribbed hose with stainless steel clamps or good quality plastic cable ties.

♦ *Outside the pond*

Use **PVC (polyvinyl chloride) or cheap polyethylene irrigation hose** outside the pond. Both materials are tough. For PVC pipes that will be buried in the garden, use the thickest grade of PVC (to resist the onslaught of rampant gardeners armed with steel tools).

The cheap plastic clamps that come with polyethylene irrigation hose become brittle from sunlight and are designed only for low pressure. Plastic cable ties can also be damaged by sunlight. For all hoses, use **stainless steel hose clamps** or at least **good quality galvanized clamps. If anything leaks outside the pond you could have a disaster on your hands** - your pond can run dry killing your fish and water plants and burning out your pump and UV clarifier globe.

♦ *Inside the pond*

For pipes to be inconspicuous in a pond, they must be the same colour as the pond walls, which look best if they are black. Polyethylene is lighter than water so it can be difficult to fix to the pond's bottom without penetrating the pond's sealant. Black PVC pipes are usually difficult to get and expensive. White PVC can be painted black but the best option by far is **black food-grade vinyl hose**. Not only is it heavier than water, it is supple and easy to work with.

If you want a really supple hose to go into awkward places without using a multitude of clumsy fittings, use **black ribbed hose**. This hose bends easily around the tightest corner. Both food-grade vinyl and ribbed hoses are expensive and soft - they are easily pierced by rose thorns and other garden nasties - so don't use them outside the pond.

Inside the pond, you can get away with using **good quality plastic cable ties** to clamp vinyl hoses. Ribbed hoses are usually very tight so they often don't need clamps. The only metal clamps to use inside the pond are **stainless steel**. Other metals release toxic ions into the water and most of them don't last long. It usually isn't necessary to clamp suction hoses inside the pond – the suction pressure keep the hoses on the fittings. Use only chemically stable, non-toxic materials inside the pond.

Chapter 3

Pond Equipment

If you buy pond equipment that is larger or more powerful than necessary, you will waste money not only on the equipment but also on the extra electricity to run it. Over a decade or two, this could come to thousands of dollars. You need to be sure, however, that it will do what you require. As pond equipment "gunks up" with slime and so on, it becomes less efficient. You will need to allow some extra capacity so that you don't have to clean the equipment too often. It is better to err a little on the overkill side than to have an unsatisfactory result.

Also, the fish density in your pond will have a bearing on the type and size of the equipment required. Species of fish also needs to be taken into account - for instance, koi are twice as polluting as goldfish, probably because they more actively stir up the sediments on the bottom of ponds.

If your requirements can be met by a pump and filter kit that includes a clear water guarantee, go for it. Then, if the equipment is correctly installed but doesn't keep the water clear, you can pass the problem back to the supplier. Clear water guarantees, however, mean just that - clear water. The pond can still become a morass of hair algae and slime.

Remember, good quality equipment will last longer than poor quality equipment. That means less time and expense wasted repairing or replacing gear that has stopped working. It also means less worry when you go away on holidays.

The main items of equipment for a pond are:

❖ *Pumps*

❖ *Filters – mechanical, biological and UV clarifiers*

❖ *Leaf skimmer*

❖ *Water features*

❖ *Underwater lights*

❖ *Copper ionizer*

Pumps

The main considerations for pumps are:

- **Submersible pumps:** In the long run, submersibles are less trouble and more efficient than non-submersibles.
- **Dirty water pumps:** These are almost maintenance free.
- **Pumps with prefilters:** Essential for most fountains.
- **Pumping efficiency:** Compare the pumping capacity of the pump against the power consumption.
- **Pumping capacity and head:** To **aerate** the pond water adequately, the pump should continuously circulate all the pond water every two hours. Also, the pump must send enough water through **water features** such as waterfalls to make them look their best. To work out which pump you need, you should be able to read a **pump flow chart**.

◆ *Submersible pumps*

The best pond pumps are submersibles because being underwater they never lose their prime so they never run dry causing them to burn out. Also, they use less power than pumps with equivalent pumping capacity placed above the pond's surface. Unlike most other pumps, submersibles are usually designed to run continuously for years. Large submersibles are expensive but a true costing of pumps should take into account their power consumption and their life span when run continuously.

The **power cost** can be estimated from the number of watts stamped on the pump. The pump must be rated for continuous running and the **period of their guarantee** should give you an indication of how long it will last. Pumps usually last up to twice the period of their guarantee. In the long run, top of the range submersibles may be the best value for money, especially if you have to pay a tradesman to replace your pump when it no longer works.

◆ *Dirty water pumps*

The best submersible pumps are high quality, **dirty water pumps** which can handle large particles. They are in a cage which keeps out particles too large for the pump to handle. As long as the pump is raised up a few centimetres (a couple of inches) from the bottom of the pond, you should rarely have to clean the cage.

A filter-less dirty water fish pond pump. *Photo courtesy of Aquatec Equipment, Maddington, Western Australia.*

A dirty water pump encased within a cage. *Photo courtesy of Aquatec Equipment, Maddington, Western Australia.*

A typical **sump pump** with a power cut-off float switch to protect the pump from burning out if the water level gets too low. These pumps can also handle dirty water. *Photo courtesy of Aquatec Equipment, Maddington, Western Australia*

◆ Pumps with pre-filters

For fountains with fine spray orifices, use a pump with a **prefilter**.

◆ *Pumping efficiency*

Pumps have their power consumption rate in watts (W) marked on the pump body, along with their pumping capacity (litres per minute or gallons per hour) and their head (the height to which they can pump). Buy the pump that gives you the most pumping for the least number of watts (unless your electricity is free). Quality pumps are expensive, but over their lifetime you will use less power than you will with cheap pumps.

◆ *Pumping capacity and head*

A pump's capacity is the amount of water it can pump in a given period of time. The pump's head is the height above the surface of the pond to which the pump sends water. Before buying a pump, work out your requirements for **aeration** and for **water features** using a **pump flow chart**:

Aeration

Fishpond water needs aerating by bringing air into contact with the water to maintain a high level of dissolved oxygen for the respiration of fish and of the bacteria in the **biological filter**. Aeration oxygenates water and reduces the levels of noxious gases in the water. The simplest way to aerate a pond is to circulate the water by running a pump. Ideally, for aerating the average pond, the pump should **circulate all the water in the pond every two hours**.

The pump intake should be placed near the bottom of the deepest part of the pond, but not right on the bottom or in time it will block up with sludge. The discharge back into the pond should be positioned so that **flow is created in every part of the pond**. For example, in a long, narrow, flat-bottomed pond, the pump intake should be at one end of the pond and the discharge at the other end.

The discharge back into the pond should ideally be through a fountain, waterfall or any other feature that breaks up the water. Breaking up the water increases the surface area of the water in contact with air allowing more aeration. **The pump should be run continuously** so that the bacteria in the biological filter receive a constant supply of oxygen and food.

Water features

Apart from circulating all the pond water in two hours, allow for the pump to be able to send the **flow you want through your water features** (waterwall, leaf skimmer and so on). If you have a large waterfall and want a rushing torrent, you will need a large pump. Unless you have a large pond, your waterfall pump will be much larger than is necessary to aerate your pond. If you only need your waterfall to run occasionally, for example, when you are actually there to see it, the most economical solution is to have two pumps. You could have a small pump running continuously, aerating the water but consuming little power, and a large pump to run the waterfall when desired. The large pump could be a sump pump or a submersible dirty water pump. Don't, however, get a pump that is far too large. Over the lifetime of the pump you will waste hundreds of dollars in electricity. Also, excessive water flow can increase algae problems such as hair algae.

Pump flow charts

The pumping capacity of pumps is marked on pumps as **litres per hour (l/hr), litres per minute (l/min), gallons per hour (gal/hr) or gallons per minute (gal/min)**. However, this is their pumping rate without any **head** (that is, pumping water only to the surface of the pond). You need to also look at the pump's head, which is marked on the pump as **"H" in metres or in feet**. This is the maximum height above the surface of the pond to which the pump can send water.

Then you need to look at the **height above the pond's surface** to which you want to pump water (for example, the height from the surface to the outlet from your fountain). You will need a pump that is rated for about twice the required height. For instance, if you are pumping to a fountain outlet one metre above the pond's surface, you will need a pump rated for two metres. This is because the volume of the water delivered by a pump reduces as the height above the pond surface increases. At the maximum height to which a pump can send water, the water flow practically ceases altogether. At half the maximum height, the flow from most pumps is reduced by nearly half. So, if you want to circulate all the water in a 1,000 litre pond in two hours and your fountain outlet is 1 metre above the surface of the pond, you should use a 1,000 litre an hour pump with a 2 metre head.

When buying a pump, get a pump flow chart. Alternatively, give the pond shop all the details of your pond and let them work it out for you. If you finish up having too much flow, you can always divert part of it elsewhere, even directly back into the pond, or throttle back the pump outlet. It will cost a bit more for the pump and you will use a little more power but if the pump fails to deliver enough water there is nothing you can do about it except install an extra pump or replace it with a larger pump.

Pump flow chart

HEAD (M)	PM15000D	PM20000D	PM25000D
7.5			0
6.5		0	6210
6.0	0	5460	8160
5.0	3960	8160	11160
4.0	6300	10860	13800
3.0	8280	12960	16500
2.0	10500	14700	19500
1.0	12960	16980	21960
0	15000	20000	25000

PONDMAX PUMP FLOW RATE IN LITRES PER HOUR

A pump flow chart for Pondmax pumps showing the flow rate of various models at different pump heads. *Chart courtesy of Aquatec Equipment, Maddington, Western Australia.*

The pond below continually had a problem with excessive hair algae. The problem was greatly reduced by decreasing the water flow by replacing the pump with one that gave only a quarter of the flow. The original pump recirculated the water every 30 minutes – far more often than necessary. Stationary algae, such as hair algae, rely on moving water to carry nutrients to them. The cost of replacing the pump will be recovered eventually from the electricity saved because the new smaller pump uses much less power than the original large pump.

Filters

The main filters used in ponds are:

- *Mechanical filters: Made to remove suspended particles from the water. The main types are gravity, pressure, and centrifuge filters.*
- *Biological filters:* Designed to use certain types of bacteria to convert toxic ammonia and nitrite to less toxic nitrate which is then removed from the water by plants, algae and some other types of bacteria.
- *Ultraviolet (UV) clarifiers:* Not really a filter, clarifiers use ultraviolet light to kill microalgae so that they can be removed from the water by mechanical filters.
- *Combination filters:* The water flows through mechanical filter media first, then through biofilter media. They often have an ultraviolet clarifier combined before the mechanical media.
- *Pump prefilters:* These filters are usually attached to the pump and filter the water just before it enters the pump.

- *Mechanical filters*

Ideally, a mechanical filter would remove everything suspended in the water, leaving the water crystal clear. However, many suspended particles, such as microalgae, are so tiny that filters fine enough to remove them would have to be enormous and be cleaned often or they would block up very quickly. Fishponds with fish and plants form an ecosystem which isn't all that clean anyway. They can be kept fairly clean and healthy without resorting to extremes so the filters used for ponds are not extremely fine.

The three main types of mechanical filters are:

1. **Gravity filters:** These filters work by water flowing down by gravity through **layers of various types of fibre, such as carpet underlay, or through open-cell sponge rubber**. The filter material (media) is laid in a filter box with **the finest layer on the bottom and progressively coarser layers towards the top**. The water feeds in by gravity from the top. The coarsest particles are removed by the top layer, the next coarsest by the next layer and so on until the water leaves at the bottom and returns to the pond. I have often seen the layers mistakenly put in reverse with the finest layer at the top. The top layer, being the finest, removes everything and quickly becomes clogged. After the top layer is clogged, the water then flows through a bypass returning to the pond without being filtered.

   The filter box should be outside the pond, hidden but easy to access for cleaning. Some filter boxes are located in the pond but this makes cleaning inconvenient. Also, when the filter material is removed to be cleaned, much of the accumulated muck washes back into the pond. If you build your own filter, take care to use non-toxic materials.

2. **Pressure filters:** These are containers of **filter media such as sand, gravel or sponge, through which the water is pumped under pressure**. They cost more than gravity fed box filters but save time on maintenance if they can be cleaned by back-flushing. Swimming pool sand filters are of this type. They are better than gravity filters for large ponds because cleaning a large gravity filter takes a lot of manual work. A word of warning with pressure filters: I have seen ones that don't do the job as well as a filter that works by gravity. Possibly the reason is that the pressure breaks up coarser material into finer particles which can pass through the filter media. Pressure filters are useful, however, because they can be hidden more easily than gravity filters and if they are set up for back-flushing they are easy to clean.

3. **Centrifuge filters:** Particles which are only slightly heavier than water will remain suspended because of the currents created by the pump and by the movements of fish. In a centrifuge filter, water is rapidly circulated creating a vortex which throws suspended particles outwards by centrifugal force. **Particles heavier than water remain behind**

while the water flows out at the top of the centrifuge. The particles remaining behind are drained from the bottom of the centrifuge. Obviously particles which are as light as or lighter than water can't be removed in this way, but usually these make up less than half of the suspended matter in the water. Particles lighter than water can be removed by having a small amount of surface water overflowing from the pond to waste or to the garden. Centrifuge filters are very efficient but are expensive.

◆ *Biological filters (biofilters)*

The decomposition of organic matter produces ammonia which is highly toxic to fish. Secretions, faeces, urine, and dead organisms (fish, insects, bacteria, algae, leaves and plants) all decay in the pond water. **Certain bacteria convert the ammonia** to less toxic nitrites which are further converted by other bacteria to much less toxic nitrates. The nitrates are taken up by plants and algae. **These bacteria need oxygen, food (ammonia and nitrite) and surfaces to which they can attach.**

If your pond has very low fish density, the pond itself and objects within the pond will provide adequate surface area to harbour enough bacteria. For higher fish densities, however, extra surface area will have to be provided.

Mechanical filters provide far more surface area than the pond provides. However, mechanical filter material is fine and clogs up interfering with the flow of oxygenated water to the bacteria. Also, when the mechanical filter material is cleaned most of the bacteria will be washed away. So, additional surface area is provided in the form of "biomedia". These are **plastic balls, gravel or anything else which won't unduly restrict water flow but which will allow the attachment of vast numbers of bacteria.**

The biomedia should be located after the mechanical filter media so that the biomedia don't quickly become clogged. Usually, biomedia are cleaned only once or twice a year. It takes up to six weeks for the bacteria to recover so ideally you should have two biological filters (or two sections in the filter) and clean one at a time. This applies especially if the pond has high fish density.

◆ *Ultra-violet clarifiers (UV filters)*

1) ***UV filters keep water permanently clear:*** Microscopic algae (microalgae) can colour water to the point where you can't see your fish. When the algae die, decomposition of the dead algae causes low oxygen levels in the water and releases ammonia and other toxic substances affecting the health of your fish. Microalgae can turn the water red, grey, brown or yellow but usually they turn it green. The water is then called "greenwater". Although chemical treatments can clear the water, the best way to keep water permanently clear is with a UV clarifier. These have a **globe emitting ultra-violet light which kills the microalgae.**

2) ***UV filters need to be set up before the mechanical filter.*** When killed by the ultra-violet light, the individual algae cells clump together to form particles which are large enough for the mechanical filter to remove. With movement caused by flowing water, however, the particles can break up and once again be too fine for the mechanical filter to remove them. Therefore, the mechanical filter needs to be immediately after the UV filter.

3) ***UV filters come in different sizes to handle different flow rates***, so make sure that you get one large enough for your pond.

4) ***UV filters need maintenance:*** The globe is isolated from the water by a sleeve of glass or Teflon. If the sleeve is glass, it will need periodic cleaning. You might need to use a weak acid such as vinegar to remove calcium deposits on the glass. Teflon sleeves can go a long time without cleaning but don't transmit light as well as glass. If the clarifier has a Teflon sleeve instead of glass, it will need to be a bit more powerful. The clarifier will therefore cost a little more and use a little more electricity.

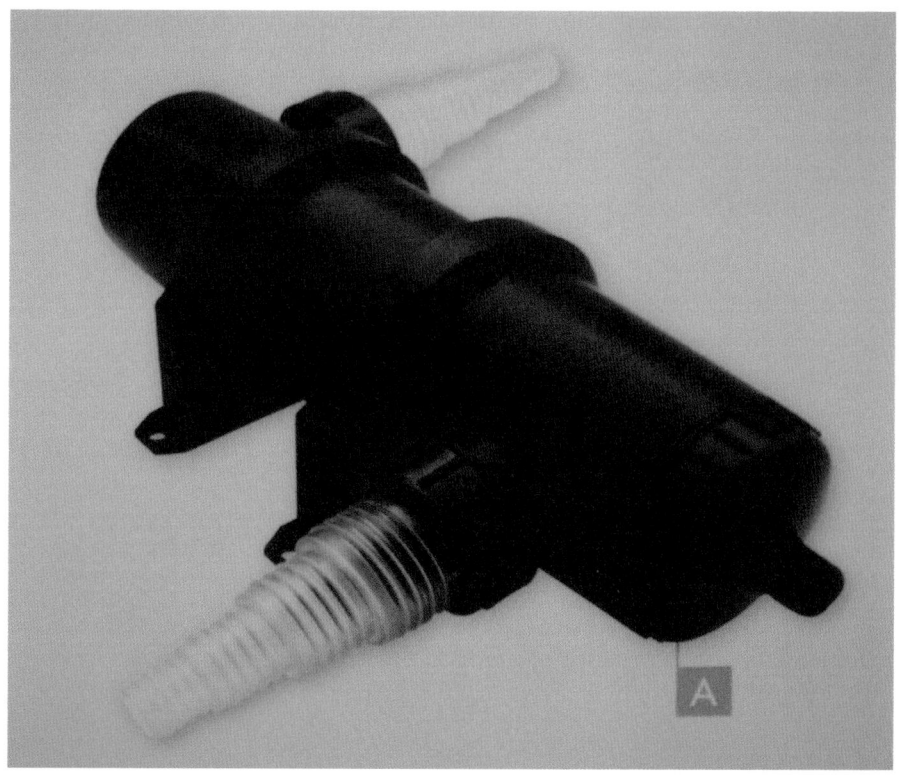

A simple UV clarifier which can be put in line before a mechanical filter.
Photo courtesy of Aquatec Equipment, Maddington, Western Australia

◆ *Combination filters*

These are simply containers, usually made of plastic, which contain both **mechanical** and **biological** filters. The water flows through the mechanical filter media first then through the biological filter media. These units often have an **ultraviolet clarifier** incorporated before the mechanical filter media. They can be gravity or pressure filters.

The following diagram shows a simple box combination gravity filter.

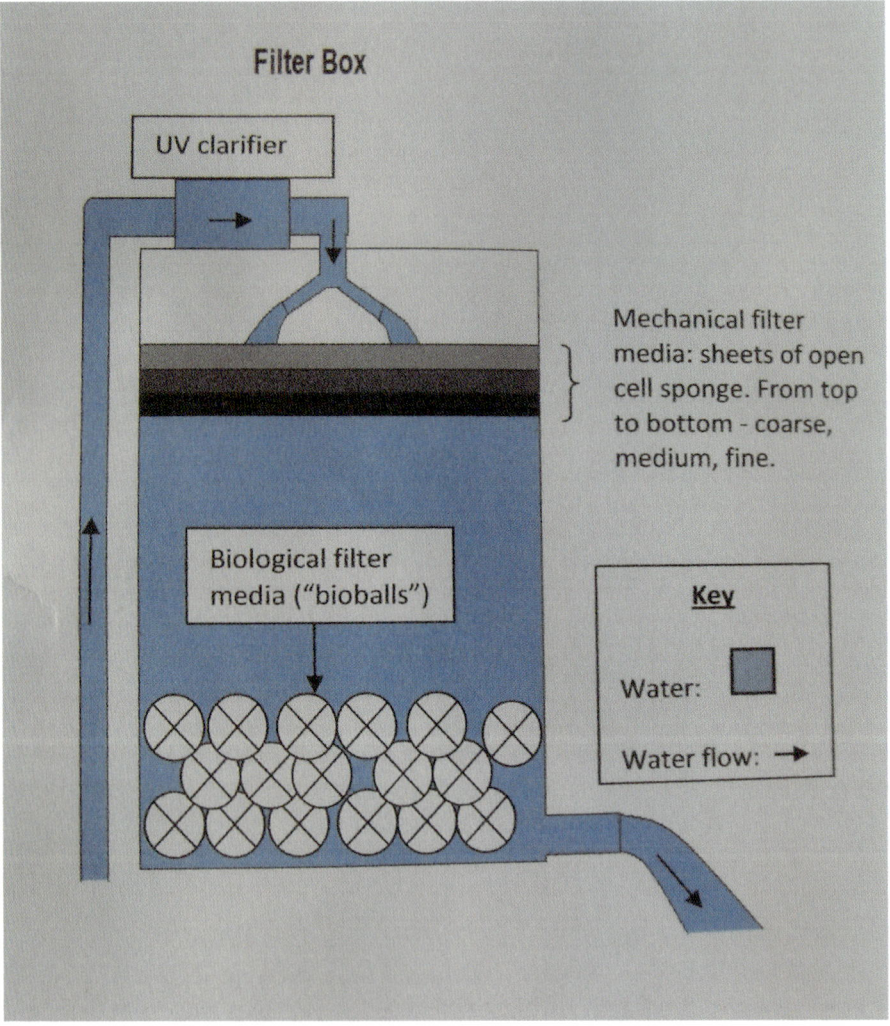

A combination UV, mechanical and biological box filter. *Photo courtesy of Aquatec Equipment, Maddington, Western Australia.*

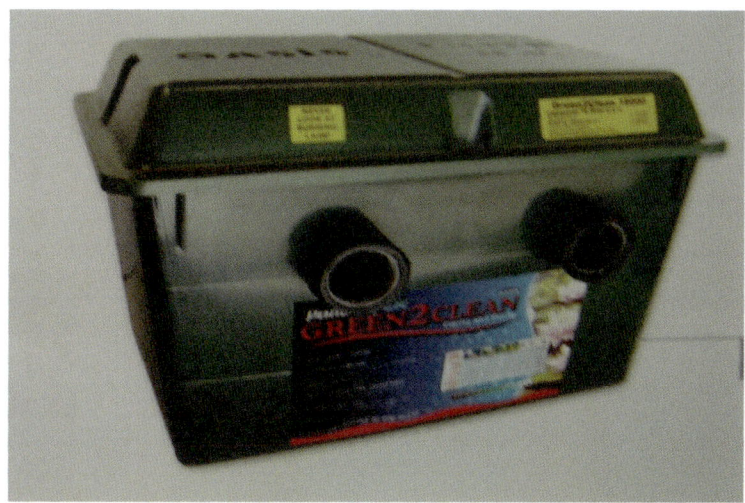

Three sizes of combination pressure filters (all have UV, mechanical and biological filters). *Photo courtesy of Aquatec Equipment, Maddington, Western Australia.*

Pump prefilters

Most pumps come with a prefilter designed to **prevent large particles from entering the pump.** Most of these prefilters are pathetically inadequate for ponds. The prefilters are suited only to small ponds, exceptionally clean ponds or to ponds with owners who enjoy cleaning the prefilter every single day. Actually, you should clean any filter daily to remove organic matter (food, faeces) before it is broken down to ammonia by bacteria, but few of us have the time to do this.

The small prefilter that comes with the pump is usually housed in a cage. The cage prevents large particles of matter from entering the filter. You can try running the pump without the prefilter. If the pump clogs up with only the cage to protect it, try putting some coarse filter material in the cage. The filter material should be coarse enough to allow the pump to run without quickly becoming blocked, but fine enough to prevent fountain orifices from blocking.

For small ponds with only a few small fish, a pump prefilter may be adequate for both mechanical and biological filtration, but not the prefilter that comes with the pump. You will need a large prefilter which is suitable for attachment to your pump. The simplest and cheapest prefilters are simply large blocks of open-cell sponge; others are boxes containing various types of filter material.

A prefilter on a threaded pipe which screws into the pump. *Photo courtesy of Aquatec Equipment, Maddington, Western Australia*

Leaf skimmers

Skimmers remove leaves by drawing water from the surface of the pond. (See *Leaf skimmers* on page 24 in Chapter 1).

Water features

Water features are more ornamental than practical but most do help to aerate the water. A huge range of products are available and it is purely a matter of personal preference which ones you choose for your pond. However, there are a few things to bear in mind:

♦ *General considerations for water features:* The feature's materials must be non-toxic. Limestone should be sealed. Unsealed concrete should be soaked for a few weeks to leach out lime. Most types of marble, granite, ceramics and terracotta are non-toxic. The only safe metal is stainless steel. Dark-coloured features look less messy than light-coloured.

♦ *Waterfalls & rapids:* Ideal for connecting dual ponds. Often it is better to have the waterfall pump separate from the filter pump. Various waterfalls and rapids are available from pond shops or you can build one in concrete on a liner.

♦ *Waterwalls:* To look good, they need a minimum water flow of 50 litres per minute for each metre of waterwall.

♦ *Fountains:* Preferably have no tiny orifices in the fountain water outlet and the pump needs a prefilter.

♦ *Urns, barrels and similar features:* To keep the water in the urn from stagnating, place the water supply outlet near the bottom of the urn. For large urns in small ponds, install a non-return valve in the water supply line to keep the pond from overflowing if the pump stops (the water might return from the urn via the pump into the pond).

◆ *General considerations for water features*

1. The supplier of the water feature should be able to give you a guarantee that the feature's materials are **non-toxic** to fish and plants.

2. If you buy a feature made of **limestone**, make sure it has been sealed with a top quality sealant. Otherwise you may find the pond's pH will remain at around 8.3. No matter how much treatment you add to bring the pH down, it will keep creeping back up to 8.3 encouraging algae growth and decreasing the effectiveness of pond treatments.

3. If you buy a feature made of **concrete**, unless it is sealed, you will need to submerge it in a tank or pond of water with no fish or plants. You will need to leave it there for at least a few weeks to leach out lime which can make the pond dangerously alkaline. Change the water after a few weeks and check the pH after a further week before risking putting it in a pond with fish or plants. To be safe, the pH should be less than 9.5 (ideally, it should be close to 7).

4. Most types of **marble, granite, ceramics and terracotta** are all right in a pond.

5. The only metal safe in fishponds is **stainless steel**. I have noticed, however, that ponds with copper and bronze statues have less algae problems (copper is highly toxic to algae). Nearly all of the ponds with copper or bronze statues which I have worked on had a pH close to 8, which is slightly alkaline. The fish appeared to be healthy, but didn't breed, so I would say that only enough copper enters the water at pH 8 to inhibit breeding. At pH 7, however, copper is far more soluble, so I would expect the health of the fish to be affected far more.

6. For a water feature I would choose **dark colours**. You can have light colours if you want all the algae and slime to give the feature a visibly "natural" character. For example, some people like the look of grey-green algae on terracotta.

◆ *Waterfalls & rapids*

If you enjoy the sound of rushing water, nothing beats a waterfall or rapid. In a **dual pond** system, waterfalls and rapids are ideal for transferring water from one pond to the other. They also add to the **aeration** of any pond.

According to pond equipment manufacturers, to keep a pond healthy, the water should be recirculated every two hours. This is a guide only, however, because conditions vary from place to place and from pond to pond. If you recirculate the water more often than necessary, you will waste money on electricity and stationary algae problems such as hair algae can increase.

Unless you want a waterfall or rapid running continuously, I would design the pond to have **two pumps**. Waterfalls and rapids need a large pump to give the desired flow. Unless the pond is large, a separate smaller pump could send water through the filters and around the pond to aerate and filter the water at the desired rate. Over the lifetime of the pond, the small pump would use far less electricity than the large pump.

I have seen numerous waterfalls and rapids built by laying down a sheet of liner and then cementing rocks together. Some succeed but others become a nightmare because the mortar holding the rocks together always seems to crack. Rocks probably have a different expansion rate from mortar when their temperature changes from night to day causing the cracks. It is extremely difficult to find and patch the leaks. If I built a waterfall, I would first **make sure the liner under the rapids forms a watertight basin draining into the pond.** Then I would pour a layer of concrete at least 100mm thick, preferably reinforced with galvanized mesh, and then **set the rocks in the concrete.**

◆ *Waterwalls*

Waterwalls are simply a wall with a trough at the top from which water flows in a sheet down the wall. To look their best, waterwalls need a minimum water flow rate of **50 litres per minute for each metre of waterwall width** (approximately 12 US gallons per minute for each yard of waterwall). Ideally, the flow rate should be double this (see the table).

Waterwall flow requirements	
Width of trough (mm)	**Litres per hour**
500	3,000
600	3,600
700	4,200
800	4,800
900	5,400
1,000	6,000
1,100	6,600
1,200	7,200
1,300	7,800
1,400	8,400
1,500	9,000
1,600	9,600

◆ *Fountains*

Fountain orifices tend to block up. Fountains should preferably have **no orifices in their water flow line less than 1 centimetre** (two fifths of an inch) in diameter. If your fountain has fine orifices, your pump will need a **prefilter.** You will also need to be able to remove the part of the fountain that contains the fine orifices to **clean** them. You should also be able to **back-flush** the water supply line on all fountains (for example, by using a garden hose).

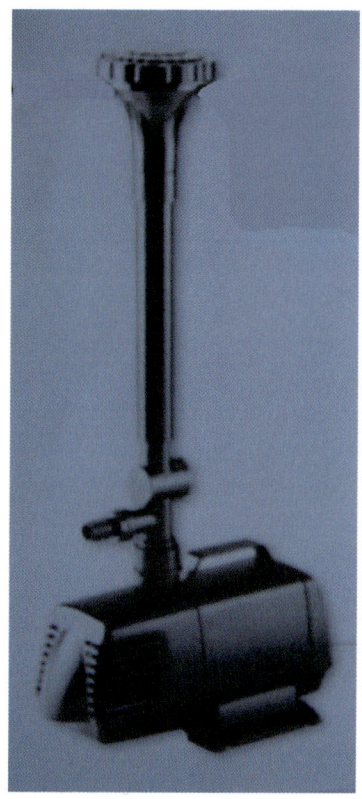

A typical fountain pump with a prefilter and a small fountain attached. *Photo courtesy of Aquatec Equipment, Maddington, Western Australia*

The fountain below has two advantages - it has a large orifice which won't block easily, and it is dark in colour so unattractive slime growing on it isn't noticeable.

The terracotta fountain above has a coarse surface to which slime algae can easily attach. The dark green slime is very noticeable against the lighter terracotta. Some people like the slime/terracotta look. The owner of this pond prefers to regularly scrub off the slime.

A "fish feature" waterspout. Photo taken at Lotus Blossom Watergardens, Baldivis, Western Australia.

♦ *Urns, barrels and similar features*

If an urn or barrel is above the water surface in a pond and the pump stops running, the water in the urn or barrel will drain back into the pond. If the urn's volume is greater than the pond's, the pond will overflow. For that reason, most urns and barrels have their water supply outlet near the top of the urn. The water in the bottom of the urn stagnates and becomes putrid (I know this because I have cleaned dozens of them). This is neither healthy for fish nor for people if the pond is inside a house. Put the **water outlet near the bottom of the container**. With urns that are larger than the pond, install a good quality **non-return valve** in the hose or pipe supplying water to the urn. Of course, even a good quality non-return valve can fail. If the pond is inside a house, the pond must be able to hold the water from the urn or drainage must exist to prevent damage to the house.

The water feature above is simply an urn placed in a small pond which has a screen across it to hold the pebbles above the surface of the water making it seem that the water flowing down the urn is disappearing into the ground. The water is chlorinated to prevent algae growing on the urn. The pump needs replacing every couple of years because fishpond pumps aren't designed to withstand chlorine.

Underwater lights

Lights are purely ornamental but can make a pond look magical at night. They come in an assortment of colours. What lights you will need is a matter of personal taste. They are usually only twelve volts so they need a transformer. My only advice is to buy quality lights and a waterproof transformer. If you have twelve volt garden lights, you can integrate the pond lights with them. That will save you the cost of an extra transformer and electrical power point.

Copper ionizers

Copper ionizers are being sold as the final solution to **hair algae** (also called blanket weed, string algae). **Copper is highly toxic to algae**. However, it is toxic only in its ionic form. A copper ionizer uses electricity to send copper ions into solution from a copper anode. When the anode is used up, it needs replacing.

According to some swimming pool websites, ionizers using copper and one or two other substances can keep the pool completely clear of algae. The dosage for swimming pools, however, is much higher than fish can endure. At the low concentration that is safe for fish, only some forms of algae are killed. The manufacturers of fishpond copper ionizers claim that hair algae is one of the forms eliminated.

The ionizers designed for fishponds probably work well in small ponds with good circulation. The ionizers that I have installed were all in large ponds and were wanting in several ways. Firstly, the construction of the units was too fragile - they were easily damaged when installed and when maintained. Secondly, they needed checking at least once a week because even split-second power interruptions turned them off so they needed reprogramming. Simple battery backup would prevent this. Lastly, copper ions rapidly drop out of solution in alkaline water. Although the ionizers were supposed to work at up to pH 8.5, I had dubious results at pH 8.

I believe that the pH of the pond probably has to be brought down close to 7 and water outlets from the ionizer need to be placed in every part of large ponds. If part of the pond has to wait an hour or two for the water carrying the copper ions to reach it, I doubt that the level of ions still in solution would be enough to eradicate the algae. You would need to increase the copper dosage to the point where the level in some parts of the pond would be toxic to fish and plants.

Ideally, for large ponds, the manufacturers of these ionizers should include probes which can be placed all over the pond. The probes should send feedback to the ionizer so that it releases ions at a rate that keeps all parts of the pond water within the optimum copper ion concentration.

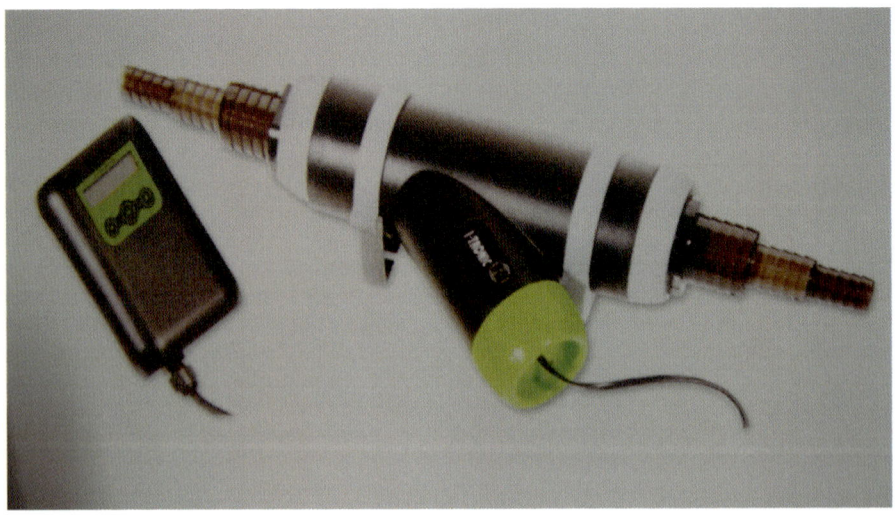

A copper ionizer. *Photo courtesy of Aquatec Equipment, Maddington, Western Australia*

Chapter 4
Fish

The main considerations for pond fish are:

❖ *Do you need fish?*

❖ *How many fish?*

❖ *What kind of fish?*

❖ *When do you put the fish in?*

❖ *Handling fish*

❖ *Transporting fish*

❖ *Feeding fish*

❖ *Fish diseases*

❖ *Fish predators*

❖ *Goldfish*

❖ *Koi*

Do you need fish?

Most fish, including goldfish and koi, eat insect larvae. You should have enough larvae eating fish in a pond to devour all **mosquito and midge larvae**. You can avoid having mosquito larvae without having fish if the water moves fast enough in all parts of the pond. Mosquitoes don't breed in moving water. If you can see mosquito or midge larvae in the pond (they wriggle up to the surface of the water to breathe) then you need fish.

How many fish?

The number of fish you can have in a pond depends on the:

♦ *reason for having fish*.

♦ *climate* of the area.

♦ *area and depth* of the pond.

♦ *water quality* in the pond.

♦ *size of the fish.*

♦ *species of fish.*

♦ *food availability in the pond.*

◆ **Reason for having fish**

If your fish are for **mosquito control**, you will need enough fish to eat all mosquito larvae in the pond. If you can see mosquito larvae, you need more fish. If your fish are for **aesthetic purposes**, it is entirely up to you how many you have, subject to the restrictions imposed by climate, water quality, size of the pond and so on .

◆ *Climate*

Fish are cold-blooded. **Their metabolism rate approximately doubles with every 10 degrees centigrade rise in temperature.** For every 10 degrees rise, fish eat twice as much and so excrete twice as much waste into the water. As a general rule, you can keep twice as many fish in water at 15 degrees centigrade as you can at 25 degrees.

◆ *Area and depth of the pond*

In a warm climate, to keep fish healthy the pond should have an average depth of at least half a metre (about one and a half feet). If the depth is less than this, the water will be too warm in summer and too cold in winter and the temperature difference between day and night will be too extreme. In cold and hot climates, the pond will need to be even deeper.

If a pond is half a metre deep but has no pump, in a warm climate, don't keep more than one 15 centimetre fish per square metre (one 6 inch fish per square yard). I have seen fish at much higher densities than this in ponds with no pump, but the chances of them remaining healthy in a warm climate are not good. With a pump and suitable filtration, you can keep a lot more fish (as explained in the following section on "water quality").

◆ *Water quality*

Water quality is the physical, chemical and biological characteristics of water. **The better the water quality, the more fish biomass you can keep.** With the right technology, such as oxygen injection, fish farms keep up to 200 kilograms of fish in a cubic metre of water (about 340 pounds of fish per cubic yard). However, as a rough guide, consider a garden pond half a metre (one and a half feet) deep, constantly in the shade, with well buffered water being pumped continuously through an ultraviolet clarifier and a biological filter. In this pond, you could keep up to nine goldfish of 15 centimetres length per square metre of pond (that is, 135 centimetres of fish per square metre, or about 45 inches of fish per square yard).

I would personally keep less than half this number so that the pond water would have plenty of leeway in the event of the pump or the ultraviolet clarifier failing. In a warm climate, if the pond is in the sun much of the day, I would reduce the number by half again.

◆ Size of the fish

Obviously, **the larger the fish, the more they pollute the water** so the less the number you can have in the pond. For a guide to how much fish your pond can take, refer to the previous section on *Water quality*. Fish growth tends to be restricted by the size of the water body in which they live. For example, goldfish can grow to more than 30 centimetres (12 inches) long. However, in most average-sized ponds, they usually won't grow to more than 20 centimetres (8 inches).

I wouldn't put large fish in a small pond. Koi need a larger pond than goldfish not only because they are larger. Fish such as koi often move rapidly about the pond and can be injured if they hit the bottom or sides.

◆ Species of fish

Some species need more space than others and **some pollute the water more than others.** For example, koi are twice as polluting as goldfish, probably because they stir up the bottom sediments more than goldfish do. Also, some species of fish are more tolerant of poor water quality than others. For example, koi can live in water that isn't pure enough for trout.

◆ Food availability in the pond

Ideally, you should keep only **as many fish in a pond as the natural food supply in the pond can support.** The amount of natural food available will vary from pond to pond. I have seen up to 30 centimetres of fish per square metre (about 10 inches per square yard) surviving well in ponds without being fed. The ponds in warm climates seem to produce enough natural food to keep this amount of fish healthy.

Ponds that are always in the shade and that don't have leaves or other sources of nutrients entering them will support less fish than this. Keeping the fish biomass down means you don't have to spend the money or time to feed them. Also, by not feeding the fish you aren't adding nutrients which feed algae.

What kind of fish?

Apart from personal likes, the things to guide your choice of fish are:

♦ *Government regulations:* to protect the **environment** and **fishing industries**.
♦ *Conditions in the pond:* vary according to **climate, size and depth** of the pond, and **water chemistry**.
♦ *Purpose of the fish:* Do you want fish for **mosquito and midge control** and do you want them to be **easy to look after**.
♦ *Condition of the fish:* When buying fish, look for **signs of disease**.
♦ *Compatibility of different species:* Piranhas with goldfish?

♦ *Government regulations*

In the past, governments restricted the importation of live fish that were considered to be a **pest to people and to their fishing industries**. For example, the Western Australian Government isn't keen to let us bring in piranhas (perhaps they feel we have enough of them in our government and industries already).

Today, **environmental concerns** are the main issue restricting what we can import. We already import quite a variety of exotic species including koi which are a strain of the banned common carp. Because koi are brightly coloured, in Western Australia, they haven't been banned along with the rest of their species, which is a bit racist, or, should I say "strainist". You need to check your **government's regulations** to make sure you won't be harbouring illegal immigrants (trust me: they are for sale in some shops).

◆ *Conditions in the pond* are related to:

1. **Climate:** Unless your pond is indoors, you will need to stock it with fish that can handle the extremes of **temperature** caused by the climate in your area. For example, tropical fish may thrive in your house but not in the winter freeze in your garden.

2. **Size and depth of the pond:** I have yet to see a shark or a whale in a pond but I have seen some very big koi in small, shallow ponds. The koi had scars presumably from grazing the sides and bottom of the pond. To keep koi, ideally you should have a large pond at least a metre deep. Koi are much more active than goldfish - they dive and move rapidly. They can easily injure themselves and often jump out of ponds with low free-board. Goldfish are ideal for small ponds especially if you prefer the slower, more graceful movements of goldfish to those of koi.

3. **Water chemistry:** Make sure the species of fish you get are suited to the water chemistry in the pond. **Different species often have different requirements** for pH, hardness, and salinity. Although salinity is seldom a problem in freshwater ponds, you should measure the pH and hardness in the pond and preferably buy suitable fish. The other option is to adjust the pH and hardness to suit the species of fish you want.

◆ *Purpose of the fish*

What do you want fish for? If you want to **control mosquitoes and midges**, you need carnivores or omnivores, like goldfish. Also, hardy fish such as goldfish and koi are **easy to look after**. They have a high tolerance for extremes of temperature and poor water conditions including low levels of dissolved oxygen, high levels of ammonia and nitrite, and daily swings in pH.

Another advantage of koi is that they help keep hair algae under control (unless they are overfed). If you want fish you can eat, you will obviously need a tasty species.

- ◆ *Condition of the fish*

When buying fish, look for signs of disease: film over the eyes or scales, parasites, blemishes, missing scales, fungus, ulcers, clumped or ragged fins, sunken eyes, scales or gills standing out, swollen or shrunken stomach, or unusual behaviour.

- ◆ *Compatibility of different species*

If you intend to put more than one species in a pond, find out first if they are **compatible**. You don't want piranhas in with goldfish.

When do you put the fish in?

- ◆ *Fill the pond* for a few days, and then **pump it out** to get rid of any toxic contaminants (if the pond is new).
- ◆ *Begin with a few small fish* to allow time for nitrifying bacteria to develop to convert fish wastes to less toxic substances.

- ◆ *Fill the pond*

Your pond is ready to go with pump, filters possibly including an ultraviolet clarifier. If the pond is new, I would fill it and let the water sit for at least a few days (three weeks if you have any new concrete exposed to the water) to **leach out toxins** such as lime. Then I would empty it (into the garden), refill it and run the pump and filters to **check for leaks**.

Run the pump for a day to **gas off any chlorine** in the water or add chlorine neutralizing treatment. If your water has chloramine in it, you will have to use the right neutralizing treatment to get rid of it. Your local pond or aquarium shop should know exactly what is required for the local water supply.

◆ Begin with a few small fish

Establish **nitrifying bacteria** in the pond and **biological filter** before putting too many fish in the pond. **The wastes from fish and decaying organic matter (leaves, plants, algae, dead fish and insects) break down into various chemicals including ammonia.**

In its "free" form, ammonia is highly toxic to fish. The ammonia is converted to less toxic **nitrite** by nitrifying bacteria of the genus *Nitrosomonas,* then to much less toxic **nitrate** by nitrifying bacteria of the genus *Nitrobacter*.

It takes up to **six weeks for nitrifying bacteria to fully establish** and they will increase in numbers only as their food supply increases. In a pond, their food is the ammonia mainly from rotting leaves and fish excrement.

The most important thing to remember is to add only a **few small fish to begin with**. **Increase the amount of fish slowly** ideally leaving six week intervals between each addition of fish. This is even more important with sensitive species of fish. If you want expensive fish, put in a few cheap ones first. Don't risk expensive fish until you are sure it is safe.

You can speed up the whole process by **"seeding" the biological filter** or the pond with nitrifying bacteria (available from pond shops). When giving a pond a total clean out you need to take precautions. *(Refer to Chapter 6: Complete clean-out* on page 120).

I have seen a new pond stocked heavily with goldfish with most of the fish dead or dying. The owners had everything correct except that they didn't allow enough time for the nitrifying bacteria to develop.

Handling fish

Things to bear in mind when handling fish include:

♦ *Stress and slime:* The less handling the better.

♦ *Out of the pond management:* Put the fish in a container of **aerated water of similar temperature and pH** to that of their pond. **Direct sunlight** can damage a fish's eyesight. For long periods, add **zeolite**.

♦ *Stress and slime*

Handling fish stresses them. Be gentle. In my experience, fish appear to be less stressed when handled by hand than by net. Use a net made of knotless mesh. Handling also removes some of the **slime that coats and protects fish** against bacteria and parasites.

♦ *Out of the pond management*

When you take fish out of the water, try not to expose them to **direct sunlight**. Without the water filtering the sunlight, the eyesight of fish can be damaged. If you aren't returning the fish to the pond, transfer them as quickly as possible into water of the same or **similar temperature and pH**. Water from the pond itself is the best to use.

Preferably the water should be in an insulated container, and kept in the shade. **Aerate** the water with an aquarium aerator or a small pump. If they are to be there for more than an hour or so, put **zeolite** in the water to adsorb ammonia. Allow a few grams of zeolite per kilogram of fish (one twentieth of an ounce per pound) for every hour.

When **transferring fish** back into the pond, you can gradually **acclimatise** them by removing a quarter of a **bucket of water** from their container and adding a quarter of a bucket of the new pond water. Do this every ten minutes until the temperature in the container is close to that in the pond. Put the container in the pond and let the fish swim out.

Another method of transfer is to put them into plastic bags and float them in the pond, but I believe this stresses them more than the bucket method.

Transporting fish

The main considerations when transporting fish are:

- *Transport water and container:* **Put the fish in strong plastic bags about a quarter full of water** from their tank or pond.

- *Oxygen:* For trips of more than an hour, fill the bag with **pure oxygen**. For trips longer than a few hours, pump **compressed air** into the water.

- *Secretions and excretions of the fish:* **Don't feed the fish** for three days before transporting them (they can survive a week or two without food). **Lower the pH to 7. Add zeolite** to the transport water.

- *Salt:* Add a small amount of **salt** to the transport water.

- *Quarantine:* Keep the new fish separate from your other fish for **at least two weeks**.

- *Float the bag* in the quarantine tank for **twenty minutes** to bring the temperature of the water in the bag close to the tank water temperature. Then **mix the water** in the bag with an equal quantity of tank water and let the bag float for another **twenty minutes**.

◆ *Transport water and container*

Transport fish in **strong plastic bags about a quarter full of water**. Fish are prone to disease if they are stressed. Take the **water from the tank or pond** from which the fish were taken so that they aren't subjected to sudden changes in temperature, pH and other things which will stress them. Seal the bag with **two rubber bands**. Put the plastic bags of fish in an esky or similar **insulated container**. For trips of over an hour, put an **ice pack** in the container to keep it cool. For a clearer picture of fish transport, *see the diagram* on the next page.

◆ *Oxygen*

The main concern for fish being transported is that they receive enough oxygen. If you are transporting fish for more than an hour, it is better to fill the transport bag with pure oxygen instead of air. For trips of a day or more, place the fish in a container filled just enough to cover the fish with several centimetres (a few inches) of water. **Connect a bottle of pure oxygen** to the water or **pump compressed air** into the water.

For small loads of fish, you can use a small compressor, such as the type used to pump up air mattresses, which can be plugged into the transport vehicle's cigarette lighter holder. Attach a plastic hose to the compressor and secure the other end in the water.

The container needs a tight lid to prevent water sloshing out, and a **vent to allow excess oxygen or air to escape** from the container. Containers designed for fish transport have baffles to prevent the water sloshing around too much.

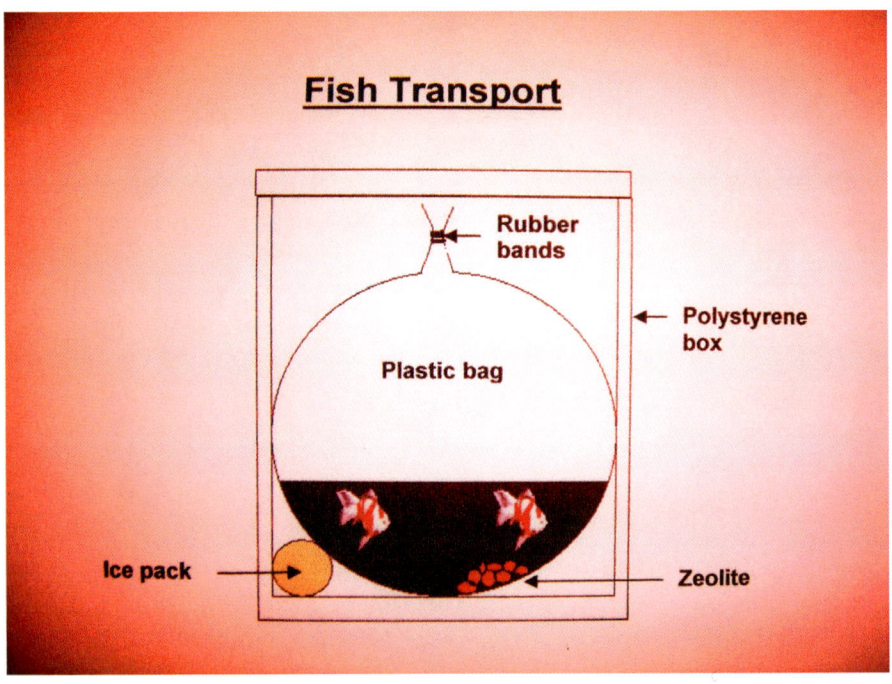

◆ *Secretions and excretions of the fish*

Remember, fish are living in their own toilet. The wastes from the fish break down into various chemicals including ammonia which, in its "free" form, is highly toxic to fish. If possible, **fast the fish** for three days before transporting them (you can safely fast goldfish for a week). While the fish are fasting, although it isn't essential, you can also **lower the pH** slowly to just below 7. Lowering the pH brings down the level of free ammonia.

The lower the water temperature, the lower the free ammonia level will be. Also, if the fish are transported in an esky with an ice pack, less ammonia will be produced because fish metabolism will be slower. For trips of more than an hour, put some **zeolite** in the bag. Zeolite is a type of clay which adsorbs ammonia. Allow a few grams of zeolite per kilogram of fish (one twentieth of an ounce per pound) for every hour of transport.

◆ *Salt*

Depending on the species of fish, up to 10 grams per litre (about one ounce per US gallon) of **salt** can be added to the transport water. The salt guards against infection which may be caused by the stress fish suffer from being transported. If you add zeolite as well, you will need to add extra because salt interferes with ammonia adsorption by the zeolite.

◆ *Quarantine*

Ideally, new fish should be **quarantined** in an aquarium tank or a separate pond for at least two weeks before putting them in with your other fish, especially if you have fish you value. If the fish are diseased, it should show within two weeks. Diseased fish should be separated immediately from the other fish and treated or destroyed.

◆ *Float the bag*

When transferring fish to a quarantine tank or pond, the water in the transport bag will probably have a different temperature, pH and so on from the tank or pond water. **Float the bag** in the tank or pond for twenty minutes to bring the temperature of the water in the bag close to the tank or pond water temperature. Then **mix the water** in the bag with an equal quantity of tank or pond water and let the bag float for another twenty minutes. Finally, open the bag and let the fish swim out. When you transfer the fish from the quarantine tank to a pond, you will need to go through this procedure again (or use the "bucket method" mentioned previously).

Feeding fish

The main considerations for feeding fish are:

♦ ***Ponds generate food for fish:*** You may not need to feed the fish.
♦ ***Uneaten food decays and pollutes the water:*** Underfeed rather than overfeed.
♦ ***Nutritional requirements of fish:*** Feed only high quality feeds. If making your own feeds, include some fish or fishmeal.
♦ ***Types of feeds:*** The easiest feed to give is pellets. The pond usually provides enough live food.

♦ *Ponds generate food for fish*

In ponds, algae and plants feed millions of organisms from microscopic rotifers and crustaceans through to insects and their larvae. If a pond has **only a few fish, I wouldn't bother to feed them** except when emptying the pond and refilling it, after cleaning it. In time, the food organisms will regenerate.

♦ *Uneaten food decays and pollutes the water*

Overfeeding fish is detrimental to their health than underfeeding them. To find out how much to feed your fish, establish a routine feeding time. Early morning and late afternoon are the natural feeding times for most fish. Once the fish have been "trained" to feed at a certain time or times, they should **consume all the feed within five minutes**.

Fish, like us, will eat more than they need, so don't feed adult fish more than once a day. To see how quickly the fish eat the food, use floating pellets or put the food where it can be seen.

If the food has excess protein, it will end up as ammonia in the water. Find out the protein requirements of your species of fish and include only as much as they require in their food (for goldfish, it is about 30% of the dry weight of the food). Try to feed **low phosphorus** food because the nutrient limiting algae growth in most freshwater ponds is phosphorus. The **digestibility of the feed** matters because any component of the food that isn't digested passes through the fish and into the water polluting it.

◆ *Nutritional requirements of fish*

The **protein, carbohydrate and fat requirements vary with different fish species**. Also, there are **specific amino acids and fatty acids which are essential for fish**. If you make your own fish food, the easiest way to supply these essentials is to include **fish or fishmeal** in the food. Keepers of aquariums often add vitamin and mineral supplements to the food, but I doubt that it would be necessary for pond fish because of the availability of natural food in ponds.

It is also important to **maintain the water hardness** preferably above 50 parts per million to make **calcium** available to the fish. Unlike us, fish don't get all their calcium from their food - much of it has to come from the water via their gills.

Usually pond owners tend to over-feed their fish. On one occasion, however, I have seen fish that were **starving**. The fish were hanging listlessly near the surface of the water as if they weren't getting enough oxygen. A few of them were lying at an angle near the bottom, rocking from side to side as if they had a swim bladder problem. One by one the fish which appeared to have the problem were dying.

Water tests showed nothing at all wrong with the water, but a post mortem of one of the dead fish showed that it had been starving. Replacing the feed with a better quality product and increasing the amount of feed and the frequency of feeding rapidly brought the fish back to life. The pond wasn't heavily stocked with fish, but it had few plants and very clear water. Although it didn't have an ultra-violet filter, it was permanently in the shade so it had **very little natural food production**.

◆ *Types of feeds*

You can make your own food but the simplest way is to buy manufactured feeds. There are two main types of manufactured feeds: **dry and moist**. Both types come in different forms but the most convenient is probably **pellets**.

Moist pellets are made by cooking or partially cooking the ingredients which makes the pellets more digestible than the dry form but lowers the content of some vitamins. The pellets will need to be suited to the species of fish you have. Some fish need **floating pellets**, others need **sinking pellets**, and some fish, such as goldfish, can be fed either.

Buy **water-stable pellets**, otherwise the vitamins and other nutrients can leach out feeding the pond's algae instead of the fish. The size of pellets ranges from 1.5 millimetres (one sixteenth of an inch) for small fish up to 7 centimetres long (3 inches) to 7 millimetres (about a quarter of an inch) for fish over 30 centimetres long (one foot).

Store feed such as dry pellets, in a cool, dry place. Some feeds need to be refrigerated or frozen. If you have a lot of fish for the size of your pond, you can add **live food** in the form of tiny crustaceans (such as daphnia) or worms of various types.

Fish diseases

The main considerations for fish diseases are:

♦ *Stress:* Most fish diseases are related to stress. The main cause of stress is **poor water quality**. The quality of the water is affected by the pond **design**, pond **equipment**, **fish stocking density, feed, pollutants** entering the pond, and pond **maintenance**. There are a few **other causes of stress**.

♦ *Quarantine and disinfection:* **Quarantine** all new fish for at least **two weeks**. If the fish in a pond have an infectious disease, **disinfect the pond, plants and equipment.**

♦ *Common diseases and their treatments:* Diseases include finrot, white spot, Chilodonella, Trichodina, Ichthyobodo (costia), velvet disease, gill flukes, fish lice, anchor worm and goldfish ulcer disease.

♦ *Stress*

Most fish disease is stress-related. The main cause of stress is poor water quality. When fish are stressed, their immunity falls. Bacteria and other parasites which are present in the water take advantage of the situation. However, if the numbers of these organisms greatly increase because the pond conditions change to favour rapid reproduction of the organisms, they may overcome even a healthy fish.

The following factors influence the water quality in the pond:

1. **Pond design:** The larger the pond and the more shade it gets in hot weather, the more environmentally stable it will be. In small, shallow ponds, **daily temperature swings** can be extreme and can affect the health of fish. If the edge of the pond is at ground level, a cocktail of **fertilizer, tree leaves, heavy metals and pesticides** may be washed into the pond every time it rains or whenever you water the garden.

2. **Equipment:** For good water quality, the right equipment is needed for adequate **aeration** and **filtration**, including **biological filtration.** The water should be aerated by circulation, spraying and turbulence. Pumping the water through features such as fountains and waterfalls is the best way of doing this. Aeration puts oxygen into the water and helps to remove noxious gases (ammonia, carbon dioxide, hydrogen sulphide, and methane). Filtration removes suspended particles and microalgae from the water. Nitrifying bacteria in the biological filter convert toxic ammonia and nitrite to less toxic nitrate which is removed by plants and algae. The fish should be introduced slowly over a period of time long enough to allow the nitrifying bacteria to establish.

3. **Fish stocking density:** This is the amount of fish for the volume of water. If your pond has more fish than the pond's natural systems and equipment can handle, the fish won't get enough oxygen and will get too much ammonia and nitrite from their own wastes.

4. **Feed:** Overfeeding fish causes pollution of the pond, not only from **uneaten food decomposing** but also from the higher levels of **secretions and excretions of the fish.** Like us, **fish will eat more food than they need** if it is easily obtained. Conversely, if fish don't get enough of the right nutrients, their immunity will fall.

5. **Pollutants:** The sources of pollutants entering the pond, apart from **fish feed**, are **tree leaves, heavy metals** in the top-up water, and wind-borne **fertilizer and pesticides**. The tree leaves will decompose, producing ammonia, carbon dioxide, hydrogen sulphide, and methane. Evaporation leaves heavy metals like iron behind in the water. Every time you top up the water to make up for that lost by evaporation, you add to the heavy metal bank in the pond. Fertilizers add ammonia and possibly other toxins to the water. Garden pesticides such as insecticides and herbicides are toxic.

6. **Maintenance:** Maintain pumps, and keep the filters clean. **Water exchange** helps control the levels of unwanted contaminants such as heavy metals and pesticides. **Maintain the hardness** of the pond water above 20 ppm (parts per million) and preferably be between 50 and 200 ppm to make sufficient calcium available to fish. Maintaining the hardness also buffers the water against pH swings.

7. **Other causes of stress:** Stress can also come from **handling, transport, constant noise and movements** around the pond, continual harassment from **predators**, or a lack of **hiding places**.

◆ *Quarantine and disinfection*

Quarantine: Some organisms, including some species of fungi, protozoans, bacteria and viruses, will attack even healthy fish. To be sure of not introducing these organisms into your pond, **quarantine all new fish for at least two weeks.** If your fish contract a contagious disease, your best option is to place them in a clean tank for treatment, and destroy those that don't respond. **Disinfect all new plants and any equipment that has been used in other ponds.**

Disinfection: Empty the pond, scrub it clean, disinfect it and let it dry for a month. Disinfect or destroy all equipment and plants (see the following *Disinfectants and disinfecting practices*). You should have a small tank for treatment of the fish and another larger tank with a biological filter to keep the fish in until the pond is ready.

When transferring fish from the pond to a tank, or from one tank to another, make sure that the pH and temperature of the new water is similar to that of the water from which the fish are coming. The easiest temporary biological filter is a large sponge prefilter set up on the pump intake. Seed the filter with nitrifying bacteria and change 25% of the water daily with water of similar pH and temperature, if possible. Run the pump continuously to maintain maximum aeration.

Before transferring the fish back to the pond, "age" the water in the pond for at least a day or two. At the same time as transferring the fish (see *Transferring fish* on page 74), move the biological filter from the tank to the pond.

Disinfectants and disinfecting practices for ponds and equipment:

1. **Simply drying a pond for a month** will kill nearly all disease organisms. However, some organisms produce cysts which are difficult to destroy.

2. **Sunlight and heat** are good disinfecting agents. Most disease organisms die at or below 60 degrees centigrade (140 degrees Fahrenheit).

3. **Agricultural lime** (crushed limestone) spread over a dry pond at a rate of one kilogram per five square metres will kill almost any organism.

4. **Chlorine** as sodium hypochlorite at 100 parts per million for 20 minutes can be used to sterilize tanks, ponds and equipment. Household bleach contains 10,000 parts per million so it needs to be diluted with water (one part bleach to 100 parts water). If you use it stronger than this or for too long, you might damage pond equipment.

5. **Potassium permanganate:** To disinfect ponds without emptying them, bypass the filter but keep the water circulating. Add 4 milligrams per litre of potassium permanganate - 1 level teaspoon per 2,250 litres (600 US gallons). If you have small fry or fish without scales, reduce the dosage by half. This will kill off bacteria, parasites, and algae including hair algae but won't harm fish or plants. It also breaks down, decomposing organic muck in the pond.

   The water will turn purple (pinkish if looked at in a white cup). When it turns from purple to brown, change 10% of the water and put the filter back on line. Repeat the whole process daily until the water stays purple for 8 hours (usually by the third or fourth day). Repeat the treatment one last time.

Most pond treatments harm nitrifying bacteria, so after treating the pond, you will need to start it off as a new pond. That is, you will need to seed the pond or biological filter with nitrifying bacteria or introduce fish only a few at a time over a period of months.

◆ *Common diseases and their treatment*

The steps to diagnose fish disease are as follows:

1. **Observe your fish:** If you spend time regularly observing your fish, you will be more likely to notice **disease symptoms**. Apart from the various unpleasant-looking changes to the fish's body, you may notice changes from normal behaviour. If you suspect that you have an infected fish you will need to proceed with the next step.

2. **Test the pond water:** To make sure the water quality is suited to your fish, test the pH, hardness, temperature, free ammonia, nitrite and nitrate levels. If you suspect a contaminant has entered the pond, for example, from pesticide sprays or runoff from your garden, you will need to send a water sample to a laboratory for analysis. If you take a water sample, it is best to get a bottle and clear instructions for taking the sample from the laboratory which will be doing the analysis. For example, if you are testing for heavy metals, do not use a glass bottle because trace amounts of heavy metals will leach into the water from the glass. If the tests don't show a problem with the water quality, proceed with the next step.

3. **Inspect an infected fish close up:** You will need to catch a fish and look at it closely, preferably with a strong magnifying glass or a dissecting microscope (stereomicroscope). Look closely at the skin, fins and gills. If you want to look further, you will need to go to the next step.

4. **Scrape samples from the suspect areas on the skin, fins and gills:** The scrapings need to be inspected under a good compound microscope. If nothing is found, samples of the scrapings can be cultivated to show if harmful bacteria are present. If still in doubt, try the last step.

5. **Surgical examination of an infected fish:** A fish will have to be sent to a veterinarian who is competent with fish. Preferably take a few live fish to the vet (see *Transporting fish* on page 74). If you are sending dead fish, keep them fresh by keeping them cool but do not freeze them (freezing fish then thawing them out ruptures the fish's body cells).

Unless fish are grown for human consumption, you can use a wide range of treatments. Your pond shop will be able to supply **general and specific treatment agents**. Infections lower immunity to disease so **secondary infections** can set in making diagnosis of the fish's symptoms difficult.

If you have difficulty diagnosing the disease, you can try general treatment agents. It is better, of course, to find out exactly which disease or diseases you are dealing with so that specific treatments can be given.

If the disease exists only in the fish and doesn't contaminate the pond, it is better to transfer the fish to a small **treatment tank** so that the natural balance of the pond isn't harmed by the treatment agents. Less of the treatment agents will be needed for the small volume of the tank than for the large volume of the pond. Also, it is easier to ensure that the water in the treatment tank is suited to the particular treatment agent being used.

For most treatments, the water should be **clean and the pH close to neutral (7)**. The water in a small tank can easily be heated to a temperature in the upper range of the species of fish being treated so that the treatment acts quickly. Fish are cold-blooded so their metabolism rate approximately doubles for a 10 degree centigrade rise. So, a goldfish treated at 25 degrees centigrade needs treating for a much shorter period than if it was treated at 15 degrees centigrade. **Aerate** the water and **don't feed** the fish. **Terminate the treatment if the fish seems distressed or to have breathing problems**.

If your fish are particularly valuable (in terms of money or sentiment), consult a veterinarian who specializes in treating fish. The following tables list common diseases, their symptoms, causes, and treatments.

For many diseases, however, the pond will need to be treated, or better still, drained, cleaned and disinfected. All plants and equipment should also be disinfected.

For details of treatments (salt baths etc.) see after the following tables.

Common Worm and Crustacean Parasites			
Disease	Cause	Symptoms	Treatment
Gill flukes	Poor water quality which encourages the rapid reproduction of flukes (tiny worms).	Rapid breathing (gill covers moving in and out quickly), rubbing against objects in the pond, "flashing". Lethargy in later stages. Flukes vary in length from microscopic to 2 millimetres (one twelfth of an inch).	Baths with potassium permanganate, formalin, or trichlorphon. Difficult to treat and very difficult to eradicate entirely. Of the most common species of flukes, Gyrodactylus, may be eradicated with only one treatment, but another, Dactylogyrus, may require weekly treatments for up to 34 weeks. Clean and disinfect the pond, plants and equipment.
Fish lice	Poor water quality which encourages the rapid reproduction of fish lice (which are actually certain species of small, parasitic crustaceans).	Rapid breathing (gill covers moving in and out quickly), rubbing against objects in the pond, "flashing". Lethargy in later stages. Small dark spots, up to 10 millimetres in width (nearly half an inch) on the skin and gills.	Formalin or trichlorphon baths, once every ten days at a water temperature above 20 degrees centigrade (at longer intervals than ten days for lower temperatures). Repeat three times. Difficult to treat and very difficult to eradicate entirely. Clean and disinfect the pond, plants and equipment.
Anchor worm	Parasitic crustaceans that look like worms. They can be brought into the pond on a fish or even as an egg on a plant.	The "worms" can be seen as long threads trailing from the fish's skin and gills. The threads can be up to 22 millimetres long (nearly an inch).	Trichlorphon baths.

Common Protozoan Parasites

Disease	Cause	Symptoms	Treatment
Chilodonella	A common parasite which can be dangerous to a fish's health even in small numbers. They feed on the skin and gills of the fish.	Rapid breathing (gill covers moving in and out quickly), rubbing against objects in the pond, "flashing". Lethargy in later stages.	Baths with malachite green, malachite green/formalin, or salt. Once is usually enough.
White spot (also called "ich" which is short for Ichthyophthirius multuifilis)	A common parasite which attacks stressed fish. The stress is caused by a sudden drop in temperature, usually overnight.	Rapid breathing (gill covers moving in and out quickly), rubbing against objects in the pond, "flashing", tiny white spots on the skin, fins and gills. Lethargy in later stages.	Baths with salt, malachite green, or malachite green/formalin. At 25 degrees centigrade, treat weekly. At lower temperatures, treat at longer intervals.
Trichodina	A common parasite which attacks fish fry and young fish.	Rapid breathing (gill covers moving in and out quickly), rubbing against objects in the pond, "flashing", white patches on the skin. Lethargy in later stages.	Baths with potassium permanganate, malachite green or malachite green/formalin. One bath is usually enough.
Ichthyobodo (costia)	A common parasite which attacks stressed fish.	Rapid breathing (gill covers moving in and out quickly), rubbing against objects in the pond, "flashing", glossy greyish-blue patches on the skin. Lethargy in later stages. Sometimes present only on the gills.	Baths with salt, malachite green, or malachite green/formalin. One bath is usually enough.
Velvet disease	A parasitic species of algae which attacks fish.	Rapid breathing (gill covers moving in and out quickly), rubbing against objects in the pond, "flashing", glossy whitish or brownish film on the skin, fins and gills.	Salt bath. One bath is usually enough. Clean and disinfect the pond, plants and equipment.

Common Bacterial Infections

Disease	Cause	Symptoms	Treatment
Finrot	Common bacteria that attack fish under stress from poor water quality.	Ragged, "rotting" fins.	Baths with salt, malachite green, or potassium permanganate, daily for a few days; antibiotics. Test the pond pH, hardness, free ammonia, nitrite and nitrate.
Ulcers	Bacteria entering open wounds.	Whitish raised patches on the skin which become red ulcers.	Direct application of mercurochrome; antibiotics. Note that ulcers caused by a bacterium called Aeromonas salmonicida (goldfish ulcer disease) can ruin fish industries - in some countries, the authorities must be notified by law. See the following photo.

Other Diseases

Disease	Cause	Symptoms	Treatment
Acidosis	pH falling well below 7 (neutral). Usually caused by the decomposition of leaves adding acids to the water.	Rapid breathing, rubbing against objects in the pond and, later, wild dashing about.	Stop feeding, clean organic matter out of the pond, exchange water, and gradually add sodium bicarbonate to bring the pH above 7.
Saprolegniasis	A water mould called Saprolegnia infects open wounds (often caused by other infections).	Light-coloured "cotton" tufts on the fish's skin or gills. Very often infects fish eggs.	Malachite green or salt bath, at 3 day intervals. Repeat three times.

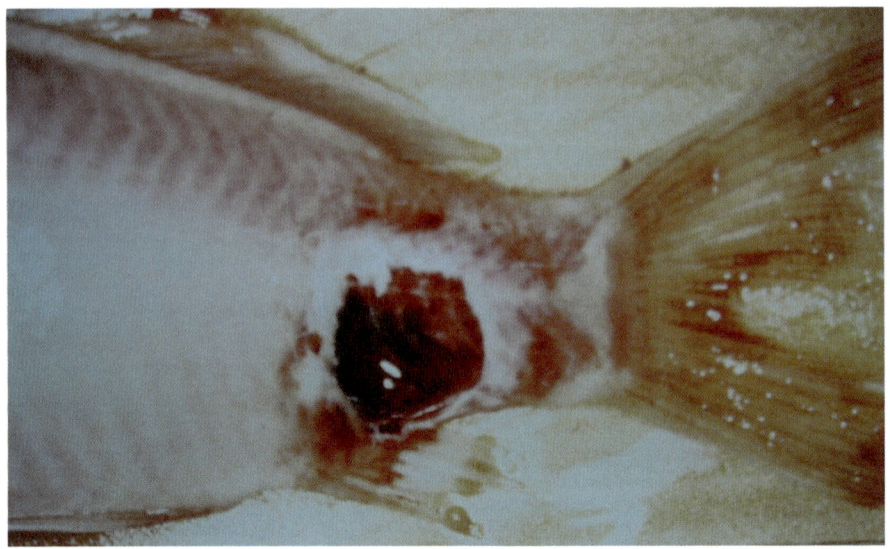

Goldfish ulcer disease. *Photo courtesy of Tina Thorne of the Department of Fisheries, Western Australia (from "Fish Health for Fish Farmers").*

Treatments:

- ◆ ***The author takes no responsibility for the following treatment recommendations.*** Treatments must be given at exact strengths for very specific time spans. If you are not confident to follow these recommendations or if you are unsure of the strength and purity of your treatment materials, contact your local fisheries, agricultural authority or a veterinarian who is competent with fish.

- ◆ For treatments that are highly toxic, dosages are given in metric units only. When you buy these treatments, make sure that you get specific instructions for handling and for calculating dosages.

- ◆ ***These treatments are recommended for ornamental fish only.*** In many countries, it is illegal to use some of these treatments on fish intended for human consumption.

1. **Salt bath:** 10 grams per litre (approximately one and a third ounces per US gallon) for 30 to 60 minutes. ***Don't use iodized salt*** – iodine is very toxic to freshwater fish. The safest salt to use is rock salt.

2. **Malachite green bath:** 0.15 milligrams per litre for ponds; 1 to 5 milligrams per litre for a 1 hour bath or 60 milligrams per litre for a 30 second bath. N.B. Malachite green is ***very toxic to humans:*** handle with care!

3. **Malachite green/formalin bath:** Add 2.3 grams of malachite green to 1 litre of 40% formaldehyde. Mix 2.5 millilitres of this solution with 100 litres of water. Treat for 2 to 3 hours. N.B. Malachite green and formalin are ***very toxic to humans:*** handle with care!

4. **Formalin bath:** Add 20 milligrams of concentrated formaldehyde to 100 litres of water. For badly damaged fish, reduce the formaldehyde by half. Leave the fish in the treatment water for 1 hour. N.B. Formalin is ***very toxic to humans:*** handle with care!

5. **Trichlorphon:** Commercial preparations of various strengths are available. Check the dosage instructions of the preparation before using it. It can be added directly to the pond to give 0.25 to 0.4 grams of active ingredient per 1,000 litres of water. After 24 hours, it becomes inactive. Repeat the treatment after 20 to 25 days. N.B. Trichlorphon is ***very toxic to humans:*** handle with care!

6. **Potassium permanganate:** Useful because it is non-toxic to humans. Can be used to treat ponds but working out the dosage is complicated because it reacts with organic matter. In a clean tank with clean water, use 2 grams of potassium permanganate per 1,000 litres of water (0.27 ounces of potassium permanganate per 1,000 US gallons of water). The water should stay purple for at least 4 hours before turning brown. If the water turns brown in less than four hours, increase the dosage. The same procedure is used for disinfecting water plants.

7. **Antibiotics:** Obtained by prescription from veterinarians. Observe dosage instructions carefully. The best method for administering the antibiotics is by injection.

Occasionally, a fish may die for no apparent reason. As long as the rest of the fish appear to be healthy, don't worry. With the aid of the **right equipment and regular maintenance**, your pond should develop a healthy ecosystem.

Fish predators

The main concerns for predators of fish in ponds are:

- *Cats and birds* are the most common predators in towns and cities. **Netting** the pond is the best defence.
- *Hiding places* are necessary if you don't want a net over the pond.

- *Cats and birds*

The main dangers a town or city fish faces are **cats and birds** (herons, kingfishers and even crows). Boys (and some girls) also poach fish but we must assume, for our own peace of mind, that they give them a good home. I have heard that frogs will prey on fish as big as themselves. In the countryside, water rats, turtles, snakes and eels are also on the prowl.

The only good protection against birds and cats is to net the pond. Steel mesh spoils the look of the pond and makes observation of the fish difficult. I have seen ponds with submerged steel mesh – the steel is usually rusted so it is releasing iron into the water. Iron is toxic to both fish and plants. Galvanised mesh eventually loses its galvanizing when it is permanently underwater. Excessive zinc from the galvanising is also toxic to fish. If you must use submerged metal mesh, make it **stainless steel**. If your pond is deep, for the safety of children strong stainless steel mesh might be necessary. My personal preference is for **fine black nylon mesh**. It isn't noticeable and if it is attached to a frame, it can be removed to observe the fish.

◆ *Hiding places*

If you hate the look of netting over your pond, then provide plenty of **hiding places** for your fish. Install hollow ornaments, stones or statues - anything that the fish can swim into or under. If you have your plants in pots raised on brick platforms, leave a space between the bricks so the fish can hide there. Plants, especially water lilies, give cover also. If your pond is covered, for example by a shaded pergola, it will be less noticeable to predatory birds.

Goldfish

The main points I will consider are:

- *Varieties:* The most popular varieties are **comets, fantails,** and **shubunkins.**
- *Feeding:* Goldfish are **omnivorous**. They need a balanced diet. You can buy prepared feeds or make your own.
- *Breeding:* Goldfish breed in **summer** if they have **fibrous material to which they can attach their eggs.**

◆ *Varieties*

Although goldfish were kept as pets in ancient China, it was the Japanese who developed the variety of shapes and colours we see today. The original wild goldfish was olive coloured and grew to more than 30 centimetres (one foot) long. The most popular varieties for pets are **comets** (orange and gold), **fantails**, and **shubunkins** ("speckled" goldfish). Comets and shubunkins probably survive better in ponds than fantails because they can move faster to get away from predators.

Goldfish come in a variety of colours and shapes. Photos taken at Lotus Blossom Watergardens, Baldivis, Western Australia.

Below, another variety of goldfish. Photo taken at Lotus Blossom Watergardens, Baldivis, Western Australia.

◆ *Feeding*

Goldfish are **omnivorous**: they eat both animal and vegetable matter. There isn't much scientific information available for goldfish diet, but there is for a close relative, the carp. If you want to make your own food for goldfish, you can probably work on about **30% protein (in percentage of dry weight), 10% fat and the rest carbohydrate**.

Young fish and breeding females need double the amount of protein but remember that excess protein ends up as ammonia in the water. You should **include some fish or fishmeal** in the mix because it is the easiest way to supply certain nutrients which are essential to fish.

A simple way to **make your own feed** is to use a blender to liquefy fish, wheat germ and vegetables then mix in gelatine and let it set. Slice it into sheets or blocks and then freeze them. Basically, use about 30% to 40% fish or fishmeal, 15% wheat germ and the rest vegetables (e.g. peas, carrots, spinach). The exact amount of gelatine needed depends on the ingredients used.

There are plenty of recipes available on the internet giving exact proportions of ingredients. Whether to cook the ingredients or not is arguable - probably the best solution is to include both cooked and raw ingredients.

You can buy prepared feeds in several forms including **floating or sinking pellets**. The advantage of floating pellets is that it is easy to see whether the fish are eating it all. They should consume all the food in five minutes. **Any uneaten food will add nutrients to the water which will increase algae in the pond**.

I have read that goldfish can gulp air when eating floating pellets causing swim bladder problems, but I have never seen any evidence of this. The main thing to remember is to buy good **quality feeds** that have the right balance of protein, fat and carbohydrate. The feed should include some **fish or fishmeal** and have a **low phosphorus** level. Good quality feeds have higher **digestibility** than poor quality feeds so they are less polluting.

◆ *Breeding*

Goldfish will breed naturally in **summer** if they have **fibrous material to which they can attach their eggs**. The roots of water plants are usually enough to encourage breeding. Although each goldfish lays hundreds of eggs, few of the young survive. Nearly all the eggs and larvae are eaten by predators such as insects, insect larvae, frogs and even the goldfish themselves. Many of the young goldfish might fall prey to birds and cats. The few survivors become adept at hiding at the first sign of danger.

Koi

A close relative of goldfish, koi are a strain of the common carp. A vast amount of research has been done on the common carp by the aquaculture industry. Keepers of koi have also supplied a great deal of information to make life easier for pond enthusiasts. Most of the information given on feeding goldfish applies also to koi and vice versa.

A female koi will lay thousands of eggs if fibrous material is available to which the eggs can stick. As with goldfish, in a fishpond few koi will survive to adulthood.

Many pond owners prefer the graceful movements of goldfish to the more robust activities of koi. Other pond enthusiasts are enthralled by the splendid variety of colours displayed by a school of koi moving in a pond.

Goldfish and koi can be kept together, but if your pond is small and less than a metre deep, koi will often be injured. They like to dive and are also prone to jumping so they need more free-board at the pond's edges than goldfish need.

To give a truly spectacular display of koi, you need a much larger pond than this to accommodate a large school of fish.

This display would look better if it included some dark-coloured fish.

Chapter 5
Water Plants

The main considerations for water plants are:

❖ *Plants shade the water*

❖ *Filtration of nutrients and contaminants*

❖ *Keep plants in pots*

❖ *Don't fertilize*

❖ *Dissolved oxygen*

❖ *Food, habitat, and predator cover*

❖ *Pests*

❖ *Types of plants*

Plants shade the water

Plants shading the water:

◆ *prevent sunlight from reaching algae.*

◆ *keep the pond cooler* during the day, lowering the rate of algae production and dampening temperature swings between day and night.

◆ *Prevent sunlight from reaching algae*

The main factor encouraging algae growth is sunlight. If you limit the sunlight by providing enough shade, the algae can't take advantage of the nutrients from the fish food, tree leaves and other things that enter the water. In a warm climate, if you insist on having your pond in the sun because you must have sun-loving plants such as water lilies, then fill much of the pond with plants. At least two thirds of the water surface should be covered by plants. The best ones for shade are floating plants. Artificial floating plants look great when you first put them in the water but they soon become discoloured and dirty looking. They do shade the water and are useful as a temporary ornament (for example, for a garden party) but real plants soak up nutrients as well as shade the water.

◆ *Keep the pond cooler*

The other effect of shade in warm weather is to keep the water temperature down during the day. As the **temperature difference between day and night** increases, fish become more stressed. Also, the rate of **algae production will approximately double for every ten degrees centigrade rise** in water temperature.

This pond is kept cool and dark by water lilies making it impossible for excessive algae growth. If you have fish, ideally you should keep part of the pond surface clear so you can observe the fish. The cooler the climate, the more of the surface you can expose. Photo taken at Lotus Blossom Watergardens, Baldivis, Western Australia.

Filtration of nutrients and toxic contaminants

The main considerations for using plants as filters are:

- *Nutrient removal:* Plants take up **phosphorus** which is usually the nutrient limiting algae growth in fresh water.
- *Toxic contaminant removal:* Plants absorb nitrates and heavy metals.
- *Plant types:* **Floating plants** and **emergents with a large biomass** are the best filters.
- *Soil types:* Plain **sand** and **especially gravel** make the best soil for ponds.

◆ *Nutrient removal*

If the main interest in your pond is to have clear water to be able to see the fish, then regard plants as **nutrient sinks**. The more nutrients the plants take up, the less that will be available for algae.

After sunlight, the most important factor encouraging algae growth in fresh water ponds is **phosphorus**, not nitrates. Nitrates are usually over supplied in fresh water ponds because microscopic cyanobacteria (blue-green algae), found in most ponds, draw nitrogen from the atmosphere. The nitrogen eventually becomes ammonia in the pond water. Nitrifying bacteria convert the ammonia to nitrates which are taken up by plants and algae. Even an ultraviolet clarifier won't get rid of all the cyanobacteria because many species attach to surfaces in the pond.

◆ *Toxic contaminant removal*

Even though you won't reduce **nitrates** to the point where algae will starve, you do need to keep them below the level that is toxic to fish. The best way of doing this is with plants. Aquatic plants also take up **heavy metals** from the water.

◆ *Plant types*

The best plants for removing nutrients and toxic contaminants from the water are **floating plants**, and **emergents with a large biomass**. You need to remove dead plant matter from the water before it decomposes, adding nutrients to the water. Submergent plants are less practical because, being underwater, they can't easily be seen when they die.

Both emergents and floating plants provide shade but floating plants get all their nutrients from the water whereas plants rooted in soil, such as emergents, get much of what they need from the soil. Many emergents can be grown in floating baskets transforming them from emergents to floating plants. Some emergents, however, have a large biomass without taking up much space in the pond. I have seen a pond kept healthy and free of algae by a single clump of tall, thick bulrushes, despite the pond being in the sun all day. Plants also release chemicals which inhibit the spread of algae.

Plants such as bulrushes have a large biomass and so are excellent for removing nutrients and toxins from water. Photo taken at Lotus Blossom Watergardens, Baldivis, Western Australia.

◆ *Soil types*

The more nutrient poor the soil in which the plants are growing, the more nutrients they will take from the water around them. So, put your plants in pots of **sand or gravel with no fertilizer** whatsoever, letting them get their nutrients only from the pond wastes (fish excrement, rotting leaves and so on). Gravel is preferable to sand because it doesn't restrict water flow as much as sand. Organic matter trapped in sand decomposes in an oxygen-poor environment producing noxious gases which spread into the water (and into the air above the pond).

If the pond is well away from the house, noxious gases probably won't be a problem. In a large natural pond, a layer of sand below a layer of gravel works well because the sand provides a habitat for anaerobic bacteria which break down nitrates. Cleaning sand takes a lot of time and work, however, so I wouldn't put it in any pond which needs periodic cleaning.

Keep plants in pots

Keeping plants in pots makes it:

- ♦ *easier to clean the pond:* Soil on the bottom of a pond makes it very difficult to properly clean it.
- ♦ *easier to treat for diseases:* You can easily move potted plants out of the pond to treat for disease.

◆ *Easier to clean the pond*

Unless you have a large, deep pond filled with plants, you probably won't get a naturally self-cleaning ecosystem that doesn't smell like a swamp - at least, not in warm climates. You will need to clean your pond from time to time. **Soil on the bottom of a pond makes it very difficult to properly clean it**. If the plants are in pots, you can easily take them out of the pond to clean it. Also, it is easier to protect plants from large fish if the plants are in pots (large goldfish and koi will dig out plants). It is easy to cover the sand or gravel in pots with **stones** (the bigger the fish, the bigger the stones). Also, the larger the fish, the heavier the pots will need to be to prevent the fish from knocking or pulling them over.

◆ *Easier to treat for diseases*

When treating water plants for disease, the water is **contaminated**. Also, some pond treatments for fish diseases may affect plants adversely. If you have your plants in pots, to treat them or to treat the pond, you can move the plants to another pond or to containers of water.

Don't fertilize

If you want luxurious plants and you have fish, it isn't necessary to fertilize the plants. It takes **only a few fish to fertilize a large number of plants**. I am not aware of any exact scientific information giving the amount of fish needed to keep a specified amount of plants fertilized. As a general guide, however, one kilogram of fish will fertilize seven square metres of hydroponic vegetables. The only nutrient that is generally in short supply in fish excrement is calcium. If the water is hard or buffered against pH swings with calcium carbonate, there will be enough calcium available.

Dissolved oxygen

You need your pump running at night, even if your pond has plants. In water, dissolved oxygen is essential for the survival of most living things, including plants. Plants respire just as we do but during the day, when sunlight is available for photosynthesis, plants produce more oxygen than they use. All water plants, especially submergents, use up oxygen from the water at night. Plants don't produce oxygen at night.

Oxygen isn't very soluble in water but adequate levels are maintained in ponds with a continuously running pump aerating the water. **The most important time to run the pump is in the early hours of the morning when the oxygen level is at its lowest.** This becomes even more important if you have several cloudy days in a row because oxygen production from photosynthesis is reduced in cloudy weather.

Food, habitat, and cover from predators

Plants provide:

- **food** for fish and for organisms which fish eat. Some species of fish are vegetarians. Many species of fish, including goldfish and koi, are omnivorous – they eat both plants and animals.
- **habitat** for fish and for organisms which fish eat. Plants provide an environment for a range of tiny, aquatic organisms, many of which are microscopic. Insect larvae, crustaceans, worms and snails all thrive among pond plants.
- **cover for fish from predators.** Plants give fish a sense of security because they provide cover.

Hardy water lilies are attractive, practical plants that provide fish with good cover from predators. Photo taken at Lotus Blossom Watergardens, Baldivis, Western Australia.

Pests

The common plant pests I have encountered in ponds are:

♦ *Aphids*

If you have fish, try washing the aphids off the plants into the pond and let your fish make a meal of them. Aphids can walk on water. If your fish don't eat them, spray them with **dilute dishwashing liquid** - the surface tension of the water will be broken and the aphids will drown. **Wash the soap off** the plants soon afterwards or they will be burnt (I leaned this the hard way). Use as little soap as possible because it contains phosphorus which will contribute to algae growth in the pond. If your plants are in pots, you can lift them out and treat them on the lawn, fertilizing the lawn as you do it. I have heard that you can mix a tablespoon of dishwashing liquid with a tablespoon of vegetable oil in half a litre (about a pint) of water making it less harsh for the plants than using just dishwashing liquid.

♦ *Snails*

Snails eat plants. Keep a few **snail-eating fish** in your pond. They will also eat any mosquito larvae. Goldfish are fine for this kind of pest control. Some species of snails also carry parasites which can infect fish, so it is best to prevent them getting into the pond at all.

Types of plants

Aquatic plants are grouped as **floating**, **submergent** (totally underwater) and **emergent** (partly above water). A healthy pond should have emergent and floating plants with no submergents because you need to periodically remove dead plant matter from the water before it decays and pollutes the pond. When submergents die and decay, they are not easily noticed. For some pond species, however, submergents are desirable. For example, *Vallesnaria* is claimed to greatly increase crayfish numbers in ponds.

The best plant varieties for your pond will depend on:

- ***the local climate:*** Different plant varieties might require different **temperature** ranges and different amounts of **sunshine**.
- ***the water conditions:*** The **salinity, pH, hardness** and presence of **contaminants** such as **heavy metals** in your pond water will determine which plant varieties will be best for your pond.
- ***the purpose of the plants:*** Do you want plants for **shade, cover from predators, food and habitat** for fish and for the organisms that fish eat, or to **remove nutrients and contaminants** from the water? Do you want to eat the plants yourself?
- ***the varieties of fish*** kept in the pond.
- ***the government regulations*** of your area.

♦ *Local climate*

Different plant varieties require different **temperature** ranges and different amounts of **sunshine**. You should talk to local pond shops and pond keepers to find out which varieties do best in your area. Some plants need plenty of sunshine but others prefer the shade.

♦ *Water conditions*

Most plants don't do well in **salinity** over one part salt per thousand parts of water, but some plants thrive in brackish water. Other plants prefer **soft water** to **hard water**. Some plants are more **tolerant of heavy metals** such as iron and copper. If your water is from the town supply, it won't be hard to find out from local pond enthusiasts which plants will do the best in your pond. If, however, you are using water from your own bore, you will probably need to test it for pH, hardness, pesticides, iron and possibly other heavy metals such as copper and zinc.

♦ *Purpose of the plants*

Choosing plant varieties for their natural **beauty** is a matter of personal taste. After all, beauty is in the eye of the beholder (just ask any blowfish). You should also decide whether you want the varieties best for fish or for water filtration. Some plants are ideal for providing **shade, cover from predators, food and habitat** for fish and for the organisms that fish eat. Other plants are great for **removing nutrients and toxic contaminants** from the water. You will generally want plants to do all these things.

The best plants for shade and predator cover are floating plants such as water lilies. The best plants for food and habitat will depend on the species of fish, but generally a range of types and varieties will provide the best environment for most fish. To remove nutrients and contaminants, emergents with a large biomass and floating plants are best. The larger a plant's biomass, the more nutrients and contaminants it can absorb. Floating plants' roots are directly exposed to the water – they draw their nutrients entirely from the water, not from soil. Certain species of plants are better at capturing contaminants such as heavy metals.

Hydroponics can be used with a fish pond. The fish above are barramundi, so both the plants and the fish are being raised as food for people.

◆ *Varieties of fish*

Some plants are toxic to fish. Also, fish such as koi will destroy most plants. If the pond has koi, you will need to install only plants that won't be destroyed by them or are in floating pots so they can't reach the plants.

The plants above are in floating pots to keep the koi away from them. Photo taken at Lotus Blossom Watergardens, Baldivis, Western Australia.

◆ *The government regulations*

For the sake of the **environment** (and for the sake of your pocket or purse, if you are caught) you don't want to be encouraging the spread of banned exotic plants. Check with your local authorities to find out which species are banned in your area.

Chapter 6
Maintenance

Maintaining good water quality is the key to a healthy, attractive pond.

The main considerations for maintenance are:

- *Maintain pumps*
- *Keep filters clean*
- *Don't overfeed the fish*
- *Keep the pond clean and exchange water*
- *Maintain the pH and hardness*
- *Control algae*
- *Pond treatments*
- *Have a maintenance routine*

Maintain pumps

The most important considerations are:

♦ *"Dirty water" pumps* are designed to be **maintenance free**.

♦ Clean *prefilters* regularly, as needed.

♦ Clean the *internal surfaces* of pumps at least once a year.

♦ Most pond pumps are easily damaged so *be gentle* with them.

♦ *"Dirty water" pumps*

These pumps are designed to be **maintenance free**, but you should wash the pump cage once a year or more often. If the flow from the pump is slowing down even though the cage is clean, open up the pump and clean all the internal surfaces including the impellor.

♦ *Prefilters*

Except for dirty water pumps, most pond pumps come with a **prefilter** in a cage attached to the pump. If the prefilter is too fine, it will quickly become blocked. If it does, you can try running the pump without the prefilter but with the **filter cage** in place. Many pumps can operate without the prefilter - the cage prevents large particles from entering the pump.
If the pump gums up without a prefilter, install a **coarse filter** in the cage or replace the cage with **a large fine prefilter**. If the flow from a pump slows down and cleaning the prefilter doesn't solve the problem, take the pump apart and scrub clean all its parts. Even a fine film on the moving parts might seriously affect the pump's performance.

♦ *Internal surfaces*

Some pumps need to be checked **at least once a year for iron and calcium build-up**. This happens particularly with pumps such as the "Platypus" type. In these pumps, the impellor doesn't have a shaft – it turns by electromagnetism turning a metal disc to which the impellor is attached. If the iron or calcium build-up continues, it can eventually jam the pump causing the electric motor to burn out. If the water has high calcium or iron content, you may have to check the pump more often.

You can remove the iron or calcium by scraping it off with a screwdriver and scrubbing it with steel wool or a pot scourer. You might need to soften the build-up by soaking it in a weak acid solution first (for example, vinegar or lemon juice). Pond shops sell a compound that removes the film of mineral which can coat the internal surface of a pump. **Any substance adhering to the pump surfaces will reduce pumping efficiency.**

- *Be gentle*

Most pond pumps are easily damaged so be gentle with them. Bolts in pumps might have left-hand threads so they tighten as the impeller spins. These bolts often screw into soft brass bushes which are easily damaged. If bolts in pumps don't easily unscrew, try undoing them in the opposite direction. When screwing in left-hand threaded bolts, don't over-tighten them because they self-tighten when the pump is running.

Keep filters clean

The main considerations for cleaning filters are:

- *Blocked filters:* If you don't clean the filters, they will **block up.**
- *Mechanical filters:* These filters remove suspended particles from water. As often as possible, they should be cleaned to remove **organic matter.**
- *Biological filters:* The biological **filter media** don't need cleaning until sludge begins to build up in the media.
- *Clean filters in unchlorinated water:* Clean all filters, especially biological filters, by rinsing them in buckets of unchlorinated water, preferably **pond water.**
- *Zeolite:* If you have a lot of fish, you might use a natural clay substance called zeolite to filter **ammonia** from ponds. Zeolite needs **recycling** periodically.

♦ *Blocked filters*

If you don't clean the filters, eventually they will become **blocked**. If the pump has a prefilter that is getting blocked, the pump outlet flow slows down. You can see this at the fountain or waterfall, or at the outflow from a box filter. If the filter media in a box filter becomes blocked, the water overflows into the filter bypass. The water won't be filtered. You can check whether this is happening by looking under the lid of the box while the pump is running.

♦ *Mechanical filters*

These should be cleaned as often as possible to remove **organic matter** before it breaks down releasing **phosphorus** and other nutrients into the water, feeding algae. Fish excrement, dead microalgae, and plant particles all build up in the filters. Ideally, you should clean the filters daily. Realistically, you should do it weekly or at least monthly.

♦ *Biological filters*

The **biological media** in filters don't need cleaning until **sludge** begins to build up in the media. The water should be filtered by a mechanical filter before it passes through the biological filter so that the biological media need cleaning only once or twice a year.

If the biological media become covered in sludge, the **nitrifying bacteria** won't have good contact with the water flowing through. They will receive less **oxygen and food (ammonia and nitrite)** from the water and will die back. Rinse the media, in buckets of **pond water**, gently so that you dislodge most of the muck but not all of the nitrifying bacteria.

♦ *Clean filters in unchlorinated water*

Clean all filters by rinsing them in buckets of unchlorinated water, preferably **pond water** from the same pond as that from which the filters came. Rinse until the rinse water is reasonably clear. Use pond water because all filters act at least partially as biological filters so it is good to preserve as much of the nitrifying bacteria in the filters as possible.

If the cleaning water is chlorinated or of very different pH or temperature from the pond water, the nitrifying bacteria may be killed off. Also, the biological media in filters are usually placed immediately after the mechanical filter media. If you clean the mechanical filter media in chlorinated water, when the media is put back in the filter, any residual **chlorinated water** will be washed into the biological media when the pump starts running.

If you do clean the mechanical filter media with chlorinated water, before putting it back in the filter housing give it a last rinse in a bucket of pond water to remove any residual chlorine.

◆ *Zeolite*

If you have a lot of fish, you might use a natural clay substance called zeolite to help **reduce ammonia** in ponds. You will need at least a kilogram of zeolite per thousand litres of pond water (about 1 pound per 120 US gallons) to make a significant difference to the amount of ammonia in the water. Several times this amount of zeolite will do a much better job (you can't overdose zeolite – it is harmless natural clay).

The zeolite adsorbs ammonia until, after several months, it becomes saturated. If the conditions in the pond suddenly change, saturated zeolite can suddenly release a large amount of ammonia back into the pond endangering fish health. I would place the zeolite in bags and **recycle them every month**. If I wasn't prepared to recycle the zeolite, I wouldn't use it.

I wouldn't scatter zeolite over the bottom of the pond (some pond shops promote this practice) unless I was going to vacuum it out again within a month.

To recycle zeolite, place it for a day in salt water of about the same salinity as seawater (35 parts per thousand – for example, 3.5 kilograms salt in 100 litres of water). The salt causes the ammonia to be released back into the water. Rinse the zeolite with fresh water before putting it back into the pond.

Don't overfeed the fish

One of the main sources of pollution in ponds is food added to the pond. Keep in mind that:

♦ *Ponds generate food* for fish.
♦ *Fish should eat all of the food within five minutes.*
♦ *Uneaten food* adds **ammonia** and **phosphorus** to the water.
♦ *High quality feeds* are less polluting than poor quality feeds.

♦ *Ponds generate food*

I am repeating information given in previous chapters regarding fish feeding because the importance of not overfeeding can't be stressed enough. Ponds generate food for fish. If a pond has only a few fish, I wouldn't feed them at all except after emptying and refilling the pond (for example, after cleaning it). After refilling the pond, it will take weeks or even months for the natural food organisms to regenerate. Ideally, you should keep only as many fish in a pond as the pond can feed naturally.

♦ *Fish should eat all of the food within five minutes*

Like us, fish will eat more than they need. To find out how much to feed, establish a routine feeding time - early morning and late afternoon are best. Once the fish have been "trained" to feed at a certain time, they should consume all the food within five minutes.

♦ *Uneaten food*

Uneaten food decays and pollutes the water. Use floating pellets or put the food where you can see it so you know whether it is all being eaten.

The pellets will need to be suited to the species of fish you have. The protein, carbohydrate and fat requirements vary with different fish species.

If the feed has more **protein** than the fish need, it will end up as **ammonia** in the water. Buy water-stable pellets, otherwise the vitamins and other nutrients can quickly leach out feeding other pond life, including algae, instead of the fish.

◆ *High quality feeds*

Much of the phosphorus and protein in cheap fish feeds isn't digestible, so it ends up polluting the pond instead of growing your fish. Always use the best quality feed you can get or make your own. Try to feed **low phosphorus food** because the thing limiting algae growth in most freshwater ponds is phosphorus.

Keep the pond clean and exchange water

The main considerations for cleaning and water exchange are:

- ◆ *Nutrients and toxins will accumulate in time* producing algae and affecting fish health.
- ◆ *Self-cleaning ponds* don't need cleaning but still need water exchange.
- ◆ *Regular siphoning or vacuuming* is the best way to maintain a healthy pond.
- ◆ A *complete clean-out* of the pond annually is the alternative to siphoning or vacuuming.
- ◆ *Bacteria and enzyme treatments* help maintain a healthy balance in artificial ponds.

♦ Nutrients and toxins will accumulate in time

All ponds need cleaning sometime. How often varies from one pond to another. **Soil and leaves** will blow in, **plants and algae** will die, **uneaten food** will decay, fish and all the other organisms, including bacteria, will **excrete wastes**. All of these things will form sludge on the bottom of the pond. From this sludge, **nutrients** including phosphorus and **toxins** including ammonia and heavy metals will leach into the water.

Water usually contains minute amounts of **heavy metals**. Also, as the water runs through copper pipes it picks up copper. Usually, copper pipes are brazed together using a filler material containing lead, so lead is added to the water as well. If the pipes are made of galvanized steel, zinc (and eventually, iron) will leach into the water. In warm weather, water evaporates leaving the heavy metals behind. Every time you top up the water, you add more heavy metals.

Pesticides and other chemicals can drift into the pond on the wind or on leaves that fall into the water. **Leaves, plants and algae decay** in the pond releasing chemicals. Some substances chemically bind with others to form compounds which may be toxic to fish. In time, any substance that doesn't evaporate can reach levels which may be toxic to fish.

Cleaning the pond gets rid of the sludge in the bottom and replaces polluted water with clean water. There are two ways of keeping a pond clean. The first is to **siphon or vacuum the sludge** off the bottom of the pond at regular intervals (weekly, monthly, or quarterly). The second is to **completely clean out the pond** once or twice a year (or at least once every couple of years).

♦ Self-cleaning ponds

Self-cleaning ponds accumulate all their wastes in **filters**. Only the filters need cleaning. The pond still needs **water exchange**, however, because toxins and nutrients will still accumulate in the water for the reasons given previously. Water exchange could be achieved by installing a **back-flushable filter or a centrifuge filter** both of which use pond water to flush the accumulated wastes out of the filter. The pond is then topped up afterwards.

Another method of water exchange is to allow a small, continuous **overflow** from the surface of the pond to flow into the garden. Allowing an overflow has the added advantage of removing floating wastes and contaminants. An automatic top-up valve can be used to continuously replace the water.

♦ *Regular siphoning or vacuuming*

Regular siphoning or vacuuming is the best method of cleaning ponds because it prevents the build-up of pollutants but replaces only part of the water causing **little disruption to the pond's ecosystem.** Depending on the condition of the pond water and on how often you clean the pond, vacuum or siphon off between 10% and 25% of the water. You might need to do it weekly, monthly or once every few months.

To **siphon** wastes off the pond bottom you need to coil a hose into the pond so that the air is pushed out of the hose. Seal off one end of the hose with your hand and pull it out of the pond and place the end below the level of the pond (this may not be possible with sunken ponds). Take your hand off the end of the hose and the water should run out. Guide the other end of the hose around the pond bottom so that it sucks up the sludge. A transparent hose is better because you can see it working on the sludge.

The simplest pond **vacuums** are cheap pond and swimming pool models which operate by attaching a garden hose to use the pressure from your water supply. Buy one from a store that gives instructions for use. The most sophisticated vacuums are very expensive and unnecessary unless you have a large pond. For information regarding replacing the water, see *Refill the pond with unchlorinated water* on page 121.

♦ Complete clean-out

If you don't regularly vacuum the bottom and exchange water, you should give the pond a complete clean-out, **once or twice a year**. Provided that your pond is ideally located and set up, you might get away with cleaning it only once every two years. If you leave it any longer than that you will probably be endangering the health of your fish.

With large, natural ponds which have flow-through, cleaning might not be necessary at all. If you have a second pond connected to the first, transfer your fish there. Otherwise, transfer them to a container filled with **water from the pond** (refer to *Handling fish* on page 73).

If you need to use a pump to empty the pond, you can use the fishpond's own pump by connecting a hose to its discharge. Don't forget to switch the pump off before it runs dry (when the pond is nearly empty, you can hear the pump sucking air). If the discharge end of the hose is below the bottom of the pond, you can switch the pump off as soon as the water starts coming out of the end of the hose and let the water siphon by gravity.

To clean the sides and bottom of the pond, simply spray them with a garden hose with enough water pressure to remove unsightly slime. If the pond walls still look disgusting or have hair algae clinging to them, you can resort to using a pressure cleaner or scrubbing brush but be very careful. If the pond has been sealed with a paint-on sealant, you may rupture it causing the pond to leak. Also, you will be removing the **biofilm** (the layer of algae, bacteria and other organisms) from the surface of the pond walls. The biofilm helps to restore the pond to its natural balance when it is refilled.

When you completely clean a pond, you remove most of the micro-organisms which help to maintain a healthy environment. If your pond has fish, the most important of these organisms are the **nitrifying bacteria**. It is far better not to clean the biofilter at the same time as the pond because it takes up to six weeks for the nitrifying bacteria to regenerate. Obviously, you should leave at least a six week gap between cleaning the pond and cleaning the biofilter.

Use buckets of pond water to clean the biofilter. When cleaning the pond, keep the filter media in a bucket of pond water in the shade until the pond has been cleaned and refilled.

Ideally, you should **refill the pond with unchlorinated water.** Use either suitable water from a bore or water that has been "aged" by standing it in an open container for at least a day or two to let any chlorine evaporate. You can circulate the water using a pump to speed up the removal of the chlorine.

If filling the pond with chlorinated water, spray the water in to evaporate some of the chlorine. At the same time add a **chlorine neutralizer** (available from pond and aquarium shops). As soon as your pump is submerged, start the pump to help **aerate** the water and to speed up the removal of chlorine.

Whenever you turn the pond pump off, the flow of food (ammonia and nitrite) to the nitrifying bacteria stops and the bacteria begin to die. Cleaning should be done as quickly as possible so the pump can be restarted. After running the pump for a day to remove chlorine from the water, you can **"seed" the biofilter and pond with nitrifying bacteria** (available from pond shops). Seeding accelerates the growth of the nitrifying bacteria.

The steps I take when I clean a pond are:

1. I put **insulated containers** in the **shade** and fill them with **pond water** to hold the **fish**. I run a small compressor to **aerate** the water. A small aquarium pump or the pond pump throttled right back will do instead of a compressor.
2. If the **filter** has to be cleaned at the same time as the pond, I rinse the filter media in the pond itself to **preserve the nitrifying bacteria** as much as possible. Then, I place the media in buckets of **pond water**.
3. I rinse off **pot plants** in the pond before I remove them and place them in buckets of pond water in the shade.
4. I start **pumping** out the water, **catching the fish** as soon as I can.
    I use a garden hose to **wash down the walls** of the pond.

5. After pumping out as much water as possible, I mop up any remaining water using a large **sponge.** Then I sweep up the **sludge.** For large ponds, I use a powerful wet and dry vacuum cleaner to remove the last of the water as well as the sludge.
6. I start **filling** the pond by spraying in the water. If the water is chlorinated, I add **chlorine neutralizer** as the pond fills.
7. I remove a **quarter of the water** from the containers holding the fish and top them up with the same water with which I am filling the pond. After about **20 minutes**, I again remove a quarter of the water and top up again. I **repeat** this process until the temperature of the water in the containers is close to that of the water in the pond.
8. Meanwhile, I transfer the **plants** back to the pond.
9. I transfer the **fish** to the pond.
10. When the pond is full, I run the pump to **aerate** the water.
11. I put the **filter media** back.
12. For ponds with a lot of fish, the next day, I **"seed"** the pond and filter with nitrifying bacteria.

This pond is shallow and the stones and fountain would need constant cleaning unless you use a strong algae treatment such as chlorine. Photo taken at Lotus Blossom Watergardens, Baldivis, Western Australia.

◆ *Bacteria and enzyme treatments*

These treatments consist of specific agents which help maintain **the pond's natural healthy balance.** In established ponds, the required bacteria probably already exist in adequate numbers. These treatments are useful, however, when ponds are drained and cleaned.

Some strains of bacteria **consume the rotting matter** in ponds, capturing the nutrients before they become available to algae. However, bacteria increase and die back in cycles, so at times the nutrients are probably released back into the water where they are again available to algae. So, you still need plants to capture the nutrients. The only real benefit from these bacteria is to more quickly make unsightly organic matter invisible.

Don't put any bacterial treatment in a pond which has just been topped up with **chlorinated** water. Even if a chlorine neutralizer is used when the pond is filled, don't add any bacterial treatment for a day or two to allow time for any residual chlorine to completely evaporate. Even tiny amounts of chlorine will affect the bacteria.

Maintain the pH and hardness

Hardness refers to the amount of dissolved minerals, mainly calcium and magnesium in fresh water. In fresh water, these minerals are usually associated with carbonate and bicarbonate which **prevent sudden pH swings. pH is a measure of the acidity or alkalinity of solutions**. pH ranges from 0 to 14: Below 7 is acidic and above 7 is alkaline.

The main considerations for pH and hardness are:

- *The best pH for ponds is usually between 7 and 7.5.*
- *The water hardness should measure at least 20 parts per million* (20 milligrams per litre) and preferably it should be from 50 to 200 parts per million.
- *Treatments to increase and decrease pH* are available from shops.

- *The best pH for ponds is usually between 7 and 7.5*

The pH of most natural freshwater bodies is between 6.5 and 9.5. Most freshwater fish can acclimatize to anywhere in this range but need time to adjust. The best pH for ponds is usually between 7 and 7.5 because the water will have enough **buffering capacity** without raising the **free ammonia** level too much or overly **encouraging algae. Buffering capacity of the pond water is the ability of the water to resist change to its pH.** Below pH 7, the buffering capacity is inadequate. As the pH rises, toxic free ammonia and algae growth increase. Algae problems seem to increase as the pH of water rises above neutral, possibly because more calcium and carbon dioxide are made available. Also, although algae control treatments are claimed to work at up to pH 8.5, I suspect that they are not very effective above 7.5.

Rapid changes in pH (called pH swings) can stress fish and so affect their health. In time, organic wastes and rainwater accumulating in the pond could reduce the pH, so you should check it once a month. **Daily pH swings are caused by photosynthesis** of algae and water plants. If you want to check the pH you should do it both as early as possible in the morning, and in the early to middle part of the afternoon.

- ***The water hardness should be at least 20 parts per million***

If your water supply hardness is above 20 parts per million, your pond will probably have enough calcium and pH buffering capacity to keep fish healthy. Ideally, the hardness should be between 50 and 200 parts per million. Fish, plants and most other forms of life require calcium to survive. Unlike us, fish don't get all their calcium from their food - much of it comes from the water via the fish's gills.

- ***Treatments to increase and decrease pH*** are available from pond and aquarium supply places.

However, **pH increasers are simply alkaline substances such as baking soda (sodium bicarbonate) and agricultural lime.** If you need to rapidly increase pH, use sodium bicarbonate. If there is no hurry, limestone, agricultural lime (crushed limestone) or shells are the safest and cheapest ways to increase pH. They increase pH buffering capacity as well and also provide fish with calcium.

Shells and limestone will usually stabilize the pH close to 7.5. A coating will form on shells and limestone so they may need cleaning or replacing at times. If using agricultural lime, add a small amount daily until the hardness is between 20 and 50 parts per million. Add agricultural lime to a container and place it in gently flowing water. Remove the excess by taking the container out of the pond. If you keep adding more agricultural lime, the pH will continue to rise until it stabilizes at about 8.3. This pH encourages the growth of certain types of algae in preference to plants. Ideally, the pH should be between 7 and 7.5.

pH decreasers are acids. Have the acid either in a sparingly soluble crystalline form which dissolves only slowly or as a weak solution which you slowly add over a period of time. So that the fish aren't stressed, the acid should achieve no more than 0.1 pH change per hour over the whole pond. Add it in an area away from fish, filters and plants where there is good water flow for mixing (for example, near the discharge from the biological filter). Muriatic acid (32% hydrochloric acid) from building supply stores can be used but I would greatly dilute it before using it.

Control algae

The main considerations for algae control are:

◆ *Types of problem algae:* The main types are microalgae, hair algae (also called blanket weed or string algae) and various types of slime algae.

◆ *Reasons to control algae:* Apart from being ugly, excessive algae can cause oxygen depletion and pH swings.

◆ *Causes and prevention of algae problems:* The causes of algae problems are usually too much **sunlight** and excessive nutrients, especially **phosphorus**.

◆ *Ways to control algae:* There are thirteen ways that I know of to control algae.

◆ *Types of problem algae*

Microalgae: This is probably the least desirable of the three types of algae. The term "microalgae" covers a large number of species of **microscopic, single-celled algae** which are suspended throughout the water column. They usually turn the water green (it is then called "greenwater") but they can also turn it grey, yellow, brown or red.

Microalgae form the primary level of food chains in most natural ponds. Like most micro-organisms, they multiply very rapidly (called a **"bloom"**) until they run out of nutrients. Then they suddenly die off releasing nutrients back into the water as they decay. This allows the algae to rapidly reproduce once again until all the nutrients are used up causing another die off to low numbers. The cycle of blooms and die-offs will continue unless the nutrients are removed.

Hair algae: Also called **string algae or blanket weed**. Several different species invade fresh water, attaching to pond surfaces, equipment and plants from which they hang like clumps of green hair. Hair algae can trap sediment, turning its colour to an unsavoury grey or brown. It looks its worst when it dies and floats around on top of the water.

Slime algae: This is usually the most difficult algae of all to control. It is a problem mainly on **water features** such as fountains and waterfalls. I have also seen it **smother underwater plants.** Like microalgae, it can be green, grey, yellow, brown or red.

◆ *Reasons to control algae*

The recurring nightmare for fishpond owners is out-of-control algae. Not only are excessive algae unsightly, they can be unhealthy for fish. They can cause **oxygen depletion** during the night in ponds without adequate **aeration**. With poorly buffered water, algae can cause **swings in pH.** For fish health, visibility in the water shouldn't be less than **30 centimetres (one foot).** Also, algae can cause water to be too murky to see fish and can leave an ugly scum on the water surface.

◆ *Causes and prevention of algae problems*

The causes of algae problems are usually too much **sunlight** and excessive nutrients, especially **phosphorus**.

Sunlight: To restrict sunlight entering the water:

1. Construct the pond in the **shade of a building.**

2. Erect a shaded **pergola** over the pond.

3. Use **water plants, not trees** to shade the water. Leaves falling into the pond turn into a rotting mess which feed algae, discolour the water and produce unpleasant odours. In a warm climate, if the pond receives a lot of sunlight, cover at least two thirds of the pond with plants.

Phosphorus: You will always have clear water if you pass it through an ultraviolet clarifier. Clear water, however, allows light to penetrate which encourages hair algae and slime algae, so you still need to reduce the amount of phosphorus in the water. Of the ways that phosphorus enters ponds, the most important are **fish feed and leaves** because they are continually introducing considerable amounts of phosphorus.

Phosphorus gets into the pond:

1. in the **soil** of water plants put into the pond.
   Solution: Put water plants in gravel without fertilizer.

2. in the **plants** themselves - as they die and decay the phosphorus is released into the water.
   Solution: Remove decaying plant matter regularly from the pond.

3. in soil and **fertilizer** that gets washed into the pond.
   Solution: Build the pond, or raise the pond, so that the top is well above ground level.

4. in **fish feed.**
   Solution: Keep only as many fish as the natural food production in the pond can support. If you feed the fish, use only low phosphorus feeds with a high percentage of digestible phosphorus. Don't give them more food than they can consume in five minutes (for more information, see *Uneaten food decays and pollutes the water* on page 78).

5. in **leaves**.
   Solution: Either install a leaf skimmer, or cover the pond with a net, or scoop the leaves out (preferably daily, before they sink and decompose).

6. in **top-up water and in dust** blown into the pond. The warmer, drier and windier the climate, the higher the evaporation rate from ponds. In time, the phosphorus will accumulate even if the phosphorus level in the top-up water is low.
   Solution: Water exchange either by regularly vacuuming the pond bottom or by periodically cleaning out the pond completely.

♦ *Ways to control algae*

Apart from prevention, methods of algae control are:

1. Moderate algae treatments.
2. Strong algae treatments.
3. Ultra-violet clarifiers.
4. Manual removal.
5. Vacuuming.
6. A complete clean-out of the pond.
7. Biological control.
8. Copper ionizers.
9. Barley straw.
10. Salt.
11. Wood.
12. Dyes.
13. Water flow rate.

1. Moderate algae treatments

Various **chemical treatments** are available to prevent or kill algae. **Treatments using natural ingredients** are a little more expensive than artificial treatments but are probably less harmful to fish, plants and nitrifying bacteria. The problem with all treatments is that you are trying to kill algae without harming fish and plants. The minimum dosage required to kill algae may inhibit plants and possibly affect fish to some extent.

A further problem is that **all ponds are different** and probably require different dosages to be effective. The dosages recommended by the manufacturers are a bit hit and miss. Without knowing exactly what conditions the manufacturers tested their products under and without undergoing extensive testing of your pond, you have no choice but to stick to the recommended dosage. All you can do is try a treatment to see if it works.

Any treatment will help control algae, but to get the best result you should strictly follow the manufacturer's instructions regarding dosage and time intervals between treatments.

If you use a chemical treatment to kill microalgae, much of the dead algae will clump together and collect in your mechanical filters. The rest will settle on the bottom of the pond. You will need to clean the filters and you should siphon or pump out as much of the dead algae on the bottom of the pond as possible. If you don't, the algae will decay releasing nutrients including phosphorus which will grow more algae.

Treatments must be **safe for your biofilter** - check the manufacturers' claims. You can bypass your biofilter, but this will starve the nitrifying bacteria in the filter. It may take weeks before the bacteria numbers get back to the optimum for your pond.

If your pond receives too much sunlight or too much phosphorus, you will struggle to keep the algae down unless you overdose with treatments, harming your plants and fish (see *Causes and prevention of algae problems* on page 127). Also, I have found most treatments have unpredictable results in ponds with high temperatures (over 25 degrees centigrade) and high pH (around 8).

2. Strong algae treatments:

In my experience in a warm climate, the only treatments that control slime algae are too toxic for fish and plants. My advice is either to consider the slime as part of the feature's charm, or have no fish or plants. If you don't have fish or plants, you can use powerful swimming pool treatments like **chlorine, peroxide,** or strong concentrations of **copper** (from algae blocks or a copper ionizer).

Chlorine

The problem with chlorine is that you need to control the dosage as you would with a swimming pool because too strong a dose damages pumps and equipment. Fishpond pumps and equipment aren't designed to withstand chlorine. If you are going to use chlorine, I would recommend using **swimming pool technology** for the pond. Peroxide and copper treatments are safer than chlorine for fishpond equipment.

Peroxide

I haven't used peroxide, but from all I have read, it appears to be safe to treat **ponds with plants and fish at concentrations up to 600 parts per million.** For ponds **without fish and plants, you can use up to 1,500 parts per million.** Peroxide breaks down very rapidly in sunlight, so add it in the evening. Also, aeration removes the peroxide from the water. Pumps aerate water, so run the pump long enough to circulate the peroxide throughout the pond (usually 2 hours) then leave the pump off for 24 hours.

If you have a biofilter, isolate it so the peroxide doesn't go through it. Personally, I wouldn't use peroxide in ponds with fish because it must upset the natural balance of the organisms in the pond. Peroxide is said to control hair algae and slime algae but, at the recommended concentrations won't effectively eradicate microalgae. You will still need an ultraviolet clarifier to eliminate microalgae.

Copper

Algae treatments for fishponds release only low amounts of copper. Algae blocks, copper ionizers, and algae treatments such as copper sulphate can all be used. The minimum amount of copper needed to control algae is 0.3 parts per million. This is close to the tolerance limit for fish. The copper will interfere with the breeding of fish, harm plants and kill crustaceans, so I would use it only as a last resort.

Algae blocks and copper ionizers for swimming pools are designed to keep the copper concentration at two parts per million (nearly seven times higher than fish and plants can tolerate). For water features with no fish or plants, this is another option to chlorine and peroxide.

3. Ultra-violet clarifiers

Microalgae blooms are at their worst in spring and autumn. If the blooms are not excessive, you might let them come and go. In warm climates, however, you will usually need to control them. The best method of control is an ultra-violet clarifier.

If the clarifier has a glass sleeve, you should clean it now and then. Also, ultraviolet globes lose their power in time. You will usually need to replace the globe every six months to two years, depending on how well the ultra-violet output of the clarifier is matched to your pond.

4. Manual removal

Using an ultraviolet clarifier to kill microalgae usually increases other problems - hair algae or slime algae. Removing the microalgae allows more light and nutrients to produce the other forms of algae. Hair algae is not as unsightly as a bad microalgae bloom, however, and unlike microalgae, it can be removed manually.

5. Vacuuming

Soft slime algae can be vacuumed from the pond if you have a reasonably powerful water vacuum. The algae keep slowly returning but eventually with regular vacuuming, and if phosphorus inputs into the pond are controlled, the slime should stop coming back.

6. A complete clean-out of the pond

In my experience, it is far more effective to give the pond a thorough clean-out than to use treatments. By cleaning it out, you remove all the **phosphorus** in the water, the decaying leaves and plant matter, the sludge, and the algae.

Slime algae can invade the whole pond. In one pond where I installed an ultraviolet clarifier and a copper ionizer, there were neither hair algae nor microalgae. There weren't enough plants to absorb all the available nutrients, so the door was left open for a particularly obnoxious form of slime algae. Slime covered the copper fountain (the algae must have been very resistant to copper, probably because of their slime coating). The algae were dispersed throughout the pond in such a manner that it looked as though a microalgae bloom was present. In the end, I had to completely drain the pond and clean it, the plants and the fountain.

7. Biological control

Hair algae can be controlled by **koi and possibly by other species of fish** (except in rapids and other places where the fish can't reach it). The key to using fish is to keep them hungry. They won't eat hair algae if you over-feed them.

Microalgae can be controlled by **some species of fish** such as certain species of Asian carps (not the common European carp). In shrimp farms in eastern Australia, **sea mullet** have been used to successfully control microalgae levels. Shrimp production increased when mullet were in the same ponds as the shrimp. The most amazing characteristic of sea mullet is that they can be acclimatized to live in fresh water. Some tiny species of crustaceans also clear microalgae, but most fish species clear crustaceans.

8. Copper ionizers

Copper ionizers were designed to destroy **hair algae** (see *Copper ionizers* on page 63).

9. Barley straw

Barley straw is claimed to be a successful natural way to control hair algae. Where hair algae are already established, I haven't had much

success with it. I have been told that it works only if it is in the pond **before the algae takes hold**. If you do try barley straw, make sure that it really is barley (some suppliers will tell fibs to get a sale). Barley straw extract, available from pond shops, is claimed to achieve the same results.

It supposedly takes a month or two for barley straw to work and needs replacing every **four months**. Put it **near the surface** (it needs light) and where the **water flows well**. Use **100 grams of straw per 1000 litres of water** (about one ounce per 75 US gallons). Put it in a **fine mesh bag** with a **small float** (a small piece of polystyrene will do). You will need to tie a **weight on a string** to keep the straw from floating on the surface. Once the straw is saturated, it will sink away from the sunlight if it doesn't have the float.

10. Salt

I'm told that salt will successfully get rid of freshwater species of **hair algae**. Salt will also kill most freshwater plants so you will need to remove them from the pond for the period of the treatment (nearly three weeks). Ideally, remove your fish and the biofilter as well. If you have dual ponds, you could treat one pond first, then the other.

If you don't have a second pond, koi and goldfish can withstand salt up to five parts salt per thousand parts water for a period of time. For other species, you will need to find out their tolerance limits because some fish die at less than one part salt per thousand parts water. You will have to change the salinity slowly so that the fish can adjust. Most plants also can't tolerate salinity of one part per thousand. The biofilter will die back but will regenerate - you won't have a problem unless the pond is heavily stocked with fish.

If you treat a pond with fish and plants, first **remove the plants and sensitive fish. Add one part salt per thousand parts of water every day for four days, bringing the total salinity to four parts per thousand.** That is, one kilogram of salt per 1,000 litres of water or one pound of salt per 120 US gallons of water. The reason for bringing the salinity up slowly is to allow fish and nitrifying bacteria time to adjust.

Leave it for **two weeks**. Make **25% water exchanges daily for five days** to get the salinity back to less than one part per thousand before putting back the plants and fish. Do partial water exchanges monthly to gradually get rid of the remaining salt.

I'm also told that you won't have hair algae problems if the **salinity is maintained at 1.5 parts per thousand.** Koi and goldfish are quite happy at this salinity and in fact have less parasite and disease problems, but most plants won't survive. Freshwater nitrifying bacteria also do well at this salinity, although it takes some time for them to acclimatize.

Another way to get rid of the algae is to **empty the pond, spread salt over all the surfaces and leave it for three days**. Pumps, filters and other equipment will also need immersing in salt water. Obviously, the biofilter will need restarting so this is not a good method if you have a lot of fish.

11. Wood

I'm told that certain types of **wood**, such as Western Australian jarrah, inhibit hair algae. I haven't tried it but it is an inexpensive exercise if you can get the necessary information for wood in your area. You will need to find out which species of wood, whether it needs to be green or dry, how much is needed and how long it lasts before it needs changing.

12. Dyes

Dyes that darken water reducing the light available for photosynthesis can help to reduce algae in the pond but they give the water an unnatural hue.

13. Water flow rate

For most ponds, the water in the pond should pass through the filters every two hours. Microalgae move with water currents so the faster you pump the water through the filters, the more microalgae you remove (providing the pond has a UV clarifier). The slower the water flow, the more microalgae flourishes. Faster flow, however, encourages the growth of fixed forms of algae such as hair algae.

Fixed algae rely on moving water to bring nutrients to them. The faster the water flow, the more nutrients they get so the faster they grow. If you have a hair algae problem, you may find it is better to slow the water flow rate down to less than the recommended two hour turnover rate. Try different flow rates to see what works best with your pond. I greatly reduced excessive hair algae in a pond by slowing the water flow to a quarter of its former flow. The pump was recirculating the volume of the pond water every half an hour – four times faster than necessary.

Reducing the water flow will decrease the aeration of the water. If you reduce the water flow of a pond with a lot of fish, you might need to increase the aeration by adding water features such as fountains, waterfalls and so on.

Pond Treatments

Pond shops sell a wide range of "cures" to pond problems, most of which are ineffective unless used consistently, accurately and in ponds with the right conditions. In my experience, the main thing keeping most pond treatments from working is the pond conditions. In a warm climate, if a pond is exposed to direct sunlight for much of the day, has a high level of nutrients, and a high pH you should change the conditions before throwing away your money on treatments.

Conditions vary from pond to pond. Different ponds might or might not react the same way to a specific treatment. For example, even identical ponds side by side, filled at the same time with the same water, will often produce different algae blooms. Also, algae blooms come and go naturally. If you treat a pond at the time when the algae bloom is ready to die off, you will believe that the treatment has worked a wonder.

Before using a pond treatment, try shading the pond, cleaning the pond and filter, and reducing the pH to 7 (neutral). When using a treatment, you need to measure it accurately and closely follow the treatment instructions. To work properly, some treatments must be applied strictly at regular time intervals (once a day, once a week and so on).

Treatments already mentioned in this book include pH and hardness adjusters, algae treatments, bacterial and enzyme treatments (including those for nitrifying bacteria), and fish disease treatments. Other treatments available include ammonia removers, dechlorinators, and water clarifying agents.

Ammonia removers: Zeolite removes ammonia but only slowly. Other products could be useful in emergency situations where the ammonia level has risen dramatically for some reason (for example, if a large fish dies in a small pond). However, it is better to change the water.

Dechlorinators: These should be used when adding chlorinated water to a pond or when refilling a pond after cleaning it. Instead of using a dechlorinator, it would be better to "age" the water before adding it to the pond. You "age" water by standing it in a container, preferably with a pump running to circulate the water for a day or two.

Water clarifying agents: Suspended particles in a pond may be too fine for your filter to remove. Various agents can be added to the pond water to "clump" the particles together to make them heavy enough to sink to the bottom of the pond or large enough for the filter to remove them. Pond shops supply agents.

If you are treating a very large pond, it will be cheaper to use finely ground agricultural limestone, alum (hydrated aluminium sulphate) or agricultural gypsum. These agents can lower or raise the pH of water and, if overdosed, can harm fish. The best way to use them is to first treat some water in a jar or bucket to determine the minimum dose needed to clear the water in an hour.

Have a Maintenance Routine

Daily

1. Check the **water level**. Evaporation can cause the water level to drop daily by up to a few centimetres (an inch or so). If the level drops more than this, you might have a leak in the pond, pipework or equipment. Water features can lose water by wind or splash. Top up the water, preferably with "aged" water.

2. If you don't have a leaf skimmer, scoop out the **leaves**.

3. **Feed** the fish, if you have more fish than the pond can feed naturally.

4. Remove **dead fish** immediately. One decaying fish can quickly poison a small pond.

Weekly

1. Clean all **mechanical filters**.

2. Remove **dead plant matter** and **hair algae**.

3. If you have a lot of fish, test for **free ammonia**, **nitrite** and **nitrate** (see the table: *Water quality standards for finfish* on the following page). If any of the water parameters are outside the acceptable levels for fish culture, clean the filters and the pond bottom and exchange 10% to 25% of the water. Cheap test kits won't be accurate, so if any ammonia or nitrite is detected at all, exchange water and "seed" the biofilter with nitrifying bacteria. If the nitrate level is too high, add more plants. Test the **pH** just before dawn and in the early to mid afternoon (ideally, the range should be between 7 and 8). If the pH is swinging far out of these limits, add agricultural lime.

4. If you have a **copper ionizer** which doesn't have battery back-up, you will need to check if it is still running according to its program.

Monthly

1. **Vacuum or siphon** the pond bottom and **exchange water** by replacing the water removed.

2. Test **hardness** (maintain above 20 mg/L by adding agricultural lime).

3. If you have a **copper ionizer**, you will need to check the anode monthly to see how long the anode lasts before it needs replacing.

Annually

1. If not vacuuming monthly, **clean out the pond completely**.

2. Clean the **biofilter media**.

3. Clean the **UV clarifier sleeve** and **change the UV globe**.

4. **Service the pump**. Take the pump apart and clean it. If the surfaces have a mineral coating, scrape it off, soak the surfaces in a weak acid (vinegar or lemon juice) or use a pump cleaning solution.

Test kits

If you are a fanatical hobbyist, you could spend thousands of dollars on the latest high-tech electronic gear that can test the water for almost anything. On a more practical level, you might want to get a basic aquarium kit for testing **pH, hardness, ammonia, nitrite** and **nitrate** (see the following table: *Water quality standards for finfish*). Dissolved oxygen shouldn't need testing if you continuously run a suitable pump.

Water quality standards for finfish: Courtesy of Tina Thorne of the Dept of Fisheries, WA, Australia ("Fish Health for Fish Farmers").

Water variants	Acceptable levels for fish culture	Levels in water where fish kills have occurred
Oxygen	Over 6 ppm. Up to 100% saturation	Less than 3 ppm. Over 100% saturation.
Carbon dioxide	1.5 to 3.0 ppm	Over 15 ppm
pH	6.7 to 8.6	Less than 4 to 5, over 9 to 10
Ammonia (unionised)	Less than 0.02 ppm	Over 0.2 ppm
Nitrate	Less than 1.0 ppm	Over 100 ppm
Nitrite	Less than 0.1 ppm	Over 2.0 ppm (fresh water) Over 20 ppm (salt water)
Total hardness	20 to 200 ppm	Over 200 ppm (Carbon dioxide excess)

Glossary

Acclimatise: To get used to. For fish, this means to get used to a change in pH, temperature or other factors of water quality.

Acidity: The amount of acid in a solution. At pHs below 7, a solution is acidic. The further below 7, the more acidic the solution. Fishponds are generally between pH 7 and pH 8, which is slightly alkaline (the opposite of acidic).

Acidosis: A fish disease caused by the water in which the fish live becoming too acidic. (For more information, see *Disease: Acidosis* in the table on page 89.)

Aerate/aeration: Bringing air into contact with water, mainly to add oxygen to the water. Aeration also removes unwanted gases such as ammonia, methane, sulphur dioxide, carbon dioxide and chlorine. (For more information, see *Aeration* on page 43.).

Aeration saturation: Aerating water can saturate it with oxygen and nitrogen. Water can be over-saturated with these gases but too high a concentration can be harmful for fish.

Aerobic: Relating to or caused by the presence of oxygen. For living things: needing oxygen to be active or living. Both aerobic and anaerobic bacteria live in ponds.

"Aged" water: Water that has been exposed to air for a period of time (at least a day or two) to "gas off" (evaporate) any chlorine in the water.

Agricultural lime: Crushed limestone.

Algae: Members of several phyla of living things in the kingdom Protista. Botanists include algae as plants but algae have many differences. Algae members include the nuisance algae of ponds - microalgae, hair algae and slime algae. (For more information, see *Control algae* on page 126.)

Algae bloom: A sudden increase in microalgae (microscopic algae).

Alkalinity / alkaline: The total concentration of alkaline substances in the water expressed as equivalent calcium carbonate. Alkaline is the opposite of acidic. In fresh water, alkalinity and hardness are usually similar because most of the alkalinity normally comes from calcium and magnesium carbonates. (For more information, see *Maintain the pH and hardness* on page 124.)

Ammonia: A compound of nitrogen and hydrogen which is highly soluble in water and is toxic to fish at extremely low concentrations. Decaying organic matter (leaves, algae, fish excrement) releases ammonia. (For more information, see *Begin with a few small fish* on page 72.)

Ammonium: A compound of nitrogen and hydrogen which is highly soluble in water. It forms by ammonia combining with hydrogen to give ammonium ions which are harmless to fish. (For more information, see *"Free ammonia"* on page 147).

Amphibian: A member of the class of animals that includes frogs, toads, newts and salamanders.

Anaerobic: Relating to or caused by the absence of oxygen. For living things: able to live in an environment which has no free oxygen. The bacteria deep in pond sediments are anaerobic. They change nitrates to harmless nitrogen but they also produce toxins such as methane and hydrogen sulphide.

Anchor worms: These are crustacean parasites found on fish. The "worms" can be seen as long threads trailing from the fish's skin and gills. The threads are up to 22 millimetres (nearly an inch) long. (For more information, see *Anchor worms* in the table on page 87.)

Anode: An electrode which gives off positive ions or accepts negative ions. In a copper ionizer, the anode releases copper ions into the water.

Aphids: Tiny insects which parasitize plants. (For more information, see *aphids,* page 107.)

Aquaculture: The culture of organisms in water including the farming of plants, algae, reptiles, amphibians and invertebrates (sponges, crustaceans and others) as well as fish.

Aquaponics: The combination of hydroponics and fish culture.

Aquatic: Having to do with water.

Arthropods: A phylum of invertebrates which includes crustaceans, insects and spiders.

Back-flush: To reverse the water flow. If you back-flush a filter, the pond water cleans the filter by washing out the material collected in the filter.

Bacterial additive: Dry powder containing dormant bacteria which become active and reproduce when added to water. (For more information, see *Bacteria and enzyme treatments* on page 123.)

Blanket weed: *See hair algae.*

Bioballs: Hollow plastic balls which have a large surface area to which nitrifying bacteria can attach.

Biofilm: A layer of algae and micro-organisms which grows on the surfaces in ponds (such the walls of the ponds).

Biofiltration: The removal of toxic ammonia and nitrite from water by nitrifying bacteria converting the ammonia and nitrite to much less toxic nitrate. (For more information, see *Biological filters* on page 49.)

Biological filter (biofilter): Any surface which harbours nitrifying bacteria. Biofilters provide enormous surface area. (For more information, see *Biological filters* on page 49.)

Biomass: The total amount of living matter in one or more organisms or in a habitat. In ponds, it is the total amount of living matter in the pond. For the plants in a pond, it is the total amount of matter in all the plants. For fish, it is the total weight of all the fish. Usually with garden ponds, for convenience, the amount of fish is given as centimetres per square metre or inches per square yard.

Biomedia / biofilter / biological filter media: Material in a filter which provides surface area to which nitrifying bacteria can attach. (For more information, see *Biological filters* on page 49.)

Blue-green algae: See *Cyanobacteria* on the next page.

Box filter: As its name suggests, it is a box (usually made of plastic) containing filter material. (For more information, see *Filters* on page 47.)

Buffered water: Water to which substances have been added to stabilize the pH in order to prevent sudden changes in the acidity or alkalinity. (For more information, see *Maintain the pH and hardness* on page 124.)

Buffering capacity: The amount of resistance to pH change.

Butyl rubber: A durable type of rubber which is the best of all materials for pond liners.

Calcium carbonate: The main compound making up limestone.

Carnivore: Meat-eating organism.

Centrifuge filter: A mechanical filter which removes solid particles from water by using the centrifugal force created in a vortex (that is, by swirling water in a circular motion to "throw" the particles out of the water). (For more information, see *Centrifuge filter* on page 48.)

Chilodonella: A protozoan parasite which feeds on the skin and gills of fish. (For more information, see *Chilodonella* in the table on page 88.)

Chloramine: A compound of chlorine used to sterilize water. It is very difficult to remove from water.

Chlorine neutralizer: A chemical which neutralizes chlorine in water.

Combination filter: A filter unit which combines more than one process (usually mechanical, biological and ultraviolet filtration). (For more information, see Filters, page 47.)

Contaminants: Any undesirable substance that enters a pond.

Copper ionizer: An electrical appliance which adds copper to water to kill algae. The amount of copper added is adjustable. Copper is toxic to algae at concentrations lower than those for fish and plants. The copper level has to be adjusted so that it is high enough to kill algae but too low to kill fish and plants. (For more information, see *Copper ionizers* on page 63.)

Crustaceans: Members of a sub-phylum of arthropods. They include crabs, lobsters, and other organisms including many very tiny species, a few of which are parasites of fish.

Cyanobacteria (blue-green algae): A group of bacteria which, like plants and algae, can photosynthesize.

Cyst: A resistant living cell that can survive harsh conditions.

Denitrifying bacteria: Bacteria which convert nitrate to nitrogen (some aquaculture engineers mistakenly use this term when they are talking about nitrifying bacteria).

Digestibility: The proportion of feed that can be digested. With fish feed, the undigested proportion is excreted into the water, polluting it.

Dirty water pump: A pump that can pump water containing large particles of solid matter. (For more information, see *Dirty water pumps* on page 40.)

Dissolved oxygen: Oxygen dissolved in water making it available for respiration by underwater organisms (for example, through the gills of fish).

Ecology: The branch of biology that deals with the relationships between organisms and their environment.

Ecosystem: A community of interacting organisms together with the environment with which they also interact (for example, a pond and the organisms living in it).

Emergents: Water plants that grow partly below and partly above the surface of the water (see also *Submergents* on page 154).

Environment / environmental: The environment is the aggregate of surrounding things, conditions and influences. For a pond, it includes the air, garden, trees etc. around the pond.

Enzyme: Any protein which helps a chemical reaction to proceed without taking part in the reaction. Certain enzymes can be added to ponds to help break down undesirable organic matter in the pond.

Filter: For ponds, anything that removes a substance from water. (For more information, see *Filters* on page 47.)

Filter media: The material in a filter which removes substances from water.

Finrot: A disease where fish fins are eaten by bacteria. *(For more information, see Finrot in the table on page 89.)*

Fish lice: Called lice, they are actually tiny crustacean parasites that live on fish. (For more information, see *Fish lice* in the table on page 87.)

Flashing: This is a fish movement involving a sudden move forward followed by a turn to one side and the appearance of rubbing one of the fish's flanks on the substrate or some other object. Repetitive movements of this kind indicate that either the fish has parasites on its body or that the water quality is poor.

Food chain: The "chain" that is determined by what eats what. In a fish pond, the chain begins with algae which are eaten by micro-organisms which are in turn eaten by larger organisms (insects, insect larvae, tiny crustaceans etc.) which are then eaten by fish, frogs, and so on.

Fossil fuels: Fuels which have formed from the remains of plants and animals (coal, oil, petroleum gas).

Fountain pump: A pump designed to deliver water to a fountain. Basically, it can be any pump which has a prefilter to prevent solid particles from blocking the fountain pipes and orifices.

Free ammonia (unionized ammonia): The part of the ammonia in water which is not bound up as harmless ammonium ions. "Free" ammonia and ammonium ions exist in an equilibrium which varies with changes in the water's temperature and pH. The amount of "free" ammonia increases as either the temperature or the pH rises. Free ammonia is highly toxic to fish. (For more information, see *Begin with a few small fish*, page 72.)

Fry: Fish between the larval and juvenile stages of growth.

Genera: Plural of **"genus"** which is a term that classifies a group of closely related species.

Gill flukes: Tiny worms that live in the gills of fish. (For more information, see *Gill flukes* in the table on page 87.)

Goldfish: A member of the carp family. The goldfish's scientific name is *Carassius auratus auratus*. In the wild, goldfish are olive/grey/brown in colour. Domestic goldfish have been selectively bred to give a range of different colours. They can live for nearly 50 years and grow to more than 4 kilograms (almost 9 pounds) but they usually live a lot less than this and reach a much smaller size. Their age and size is limited by the size of the pond in which they live. (For more information, see *Goldfish* on page 93.)

Goldfish ulcer disease: A very serious and highly contagious disease caused by bacteria called Aeromonas salmonicida which cause ulcers on many species of fish besides goldfish. (For more information, see *Ulcers* in the table on page 89 and the *goldfish ulcer disease photo* on page 90.)

Gram: The metric unit of mass. There are 28.35 grams in one ounce.

Gravity filter: Any filter through which water passes by gravity, not by pumping. (For more information, see *gravity filters* on page 48.)

Greenwater: Water turned green by microalgae. (For more information, see *Microalgae* on page 94.)

Greenhouse Effect: The warming of the earth's surface caused by gases in the atmosphere which are absorbing and releasing infrared radiation from sunlight. The Greenhouse Effect has been increased over the last 160 years by the use of fossil fuels which have released gases containing carbon (carbon dioxide, methane) into the atmosphere. The carbon from dead plants and animals that has been accumulating underground for millions of years is suddenly being released into the atmosphere.

Habitat: The place where an animal or plant lives (for example, a plant in a pond).

Hair algae: A common name for several closely related forms of filamentous green algae. It is also called "string algae" or "blanket weed". In fresh water, the common genera are Spirogyra, Mougeotia and Zygnema. Hair algae often grow to excess in ponds spoiling the look of the ponds. (For more information, see *Hair algae* on page 94.)

Hardness / total hardness: The amount of dissolved minerals in water. In fresh water, hardness usually consists mainly of the total amount of calcium and magnesium dissolved in the water. It is expressed as milligrams per litre of equivalent calcium carbonate. (For more information, see *Maintain the pH and hardness* on page 92.)

Head: *See Pump head* on page 112.

Heavy metal: A metal with a density greater than five times that of water. The term includes iron, copper, zinc, cadmium, mercury and lead. Heavy metals can accumulate in animal tissues, including those of fish, until they reach toxic levels.

Hydroponics: Growing plants with their roots in water, not soil.

Ichthyobodo (costia): A protozoan which, in large numbers, become parasites on the skin and gills of fish. (For more information, see *Ichthyobodo* in the table on page 64.)

Ion/ionic: Ions are atoms or molecules which carry an electrical charge.

Impellor: The part of a pump which pushes water through the pump housing.

Invertebrates: Animals without backbones.

Koi: Brightly coloured carp of the same species as the common European carp (scientific name: *Cyprinus carpio*). (For more information, see *Koi* on page 71.)

Larva (plural: larvae): The young stage of insects, fish and some other organisms before they change (metamorphose) into the adult form.

Leaf skimmer: A device consisting of a pump inside a container positioned at the surface of a pond or pool so that the pump draws water carrying floating leaves into a strainer basket inside the container. (For more information, see *Leaf skimmers* on page 15.)

Liner: A sheet of any waterproof material used to line a pond. Usually, they are made from rubber or a type of plastic (For more information, see *Liners* on page 24.)

Litre: The metric unit of volume. One US gallon has 3.785 litres and one British gallon holds 4.546 litres. One litre is equal to about 35 fluid ounces.

Maximum water flow: The flow a pump gives when the water's head is zero.

Mechanical filter: Any filter which physically removes suspended particles from water. (For more information, see mechanical filters.)

Mechanical filter media: The material in a mechanical filter which removes suspended particles from water.

Metabolism: All the life processes of an organism.

Microalgae: Microscopic forms of algae, including those which cause "greenwater". (For more information, see *Microalgae* on page 126.)

Microalgae bloom: A sudden dramatic increase in microalgae.

Micro-organisms: Organisms so small they need to be magnified to be visible. They include viruses, bacteria, and protozoans (including single-celled algae).

Natural balance: A balance of all of the natural factors in an environment.

Nitrate: A compound of nitrogen and oxygen which is highly soluble in water and is toxic to fish only at fairly high concentrations. Nitrates are a nutrient for plants and algae. Nitrates are produced in ponds by nitrifying bacteria converting nitrite. (For more information, see *Begin with a few small fish* on page 72.)

Nitrifying bacteria: Bacteria that convert ammonia to nitrite and nitrite to nitrate. (For more information, see *Begin with a few small fish* on page 72.)

Nitrite: A compound of nitrogen and oxygen which is highly soluble in water and is toxic to fish at low concentrations. Nitrite is produced in ponds by nitrifying bacteria (see above) converting ammonia. (For more information, see *Begin with a few small fish* on page 72)

Nitrobacter bacteria: The genus of bacteria which converts nitrite to nitrate. (For more information, see *Begin with a few small fish* on page 72.)

Nitrogenous compounds: Compounds containing nitrogen such as ammonia, nitrites and nitrates.

Nitrosomonas bacteria: The bacteria which convert ammonia to nitrite. (For more information, see *Begin with a few small fish* on page 72.)

Non-return valve: A valve placed in a water line to prevent water returning to the place from which it came.

Nutrient: Any substance necessary for the life and health of living things, including minerals, vitamins, oils, fats, proteins, sugars and carbohydrates.

Omnivore/omnivorous: An omnivore is an animal that eats both plants and animals.

Organic matter: In relation to fishponds, matter of or from living things.

Oxygenation: For ponds, this means adding oxygen to water, usually by aerating the water.

ppt (parts per thousand): The number of parts of a substance in a thousand parts of solution. For example, seawater is approximately 35 parts salt per thousand parts solution (that is, there is about 35 kilograms of salt in a thousand kilograms of seawater).

ppm (parts per million): The number of parts of a substance in a million parts of the solution. For example, dissolved oxygen in water is usually less than 14 parts oxygen per million parts solution (that is, there is usually less than 14 milligrams of oxygen in a litre of water).

Peroxide: Hydrogen peroxide, a chemical which can be used to eradicate algae from ponds. (For more information, see *Peroxide* on page 131.)

pH: A measure of the acidity or alkalinity of water. pH ranges from 0 to 14, with 7 being neutral. Below 7, acidity increases exponentially and above 7, alkalinity increases exponentially. (For more information, see *Maintain the pH and hardness* on page 124.)

pH decreasers: are acids. If water is too alkaline (that is, its pH is well above 7) you can make it less alkaline by adding an acid to neutralize some of the alkalinity. (For more information, see *Maintain the pH and hardness* on page 124.)

pH swings: Rapid changes in the pH of water. In ponds, it is usually caused by the photosynthesis of algae and water plants removing carbon dioxide from the water making it more alkaline during the day. At night, photosynthesis ceases so carbon dioxide increases (from the respiration of all the living things in the pond) making the pH of the water more acidic.

Phosphate: A compound of phosphorus and oxygen which is readily taken up and used as a nutrient by algae and plants.

Phosphorus: An essential element for animal, plant and algae growth. In fresh water ponds, phosphorus is usually the nutrient that limits the growth of algae and plants. So, phosphorus is the most important nutrient to control in order to limit algae growth. (For more information, see *Phosphorus* on page 128.)

Photosynthesis: The making of organic matter by plants, algae and certain other organisms by using sunlight, carbon dioxide, water and minerals.

Phylum: (Plural "**phyla**") a division of one of the kingdoms into which life is classified.

Polyethylene: A type of plastic used for making water hose for farms, gardens and so on. It is also used to make pond liners and preformed ponds.

Polypropylene: A type of plastic used for making pond liners.

Predator: Any animal that hunts prey (including fish that hunt and kill insects, crustaceans or other fish).

Prefilter: A filter which is attached to the suction side of a pump in order to remove solid particles from the water so that they don't interfere with the working of the pump. (For more information, see *Pump prefilters* on page 54.)

Pressure filter: A filter through which water is pumped under pressure. (For more information, see *Pressure filters* on page 48.)

Protista: One of the kingdoms of living things. It includes algae, amoebas, ciliates, slime moulds, water moulds and a number of other forms of life.

Protozoans: Members of the kingdom Protista (see above) with animal-like behaviour.

Pumping capacity: The amount of water a pump can deliver in a given time (usually stated as litres or gallons per hour).

Pumping efficiency: The amount of power used for the volume of water pumped.

Pump head: The height to which a pump delivers water. With pumps submersed in a pond, it is the height above the surface of the pond to which the pump delivers water. (For more information, see *Pump flow charts* on page 45.)

PVC: Abbreviation for poly vinyl chloride: a type of plastic used to make water pipes.

Quarantine: Isolation of an organism (fish, plant etc.) to prevent the spread of disease. (For more information, see *Quarantine* on page 77.)

Rotifer: Tiny organisms which make up part of the food chain in ponds.

Salinity: The amount of salt dissolved in water, usually given as parts per thousand. (For example, seawater has a salinity of about 35 parts per thousand).

Saprolegniasis: A disease caused by the water mould called *Saprolegnia* infecting open wounds on fish. The eggs of fish are often infected by this mould. (For more information, see *Saprolegniasis* in the table on page 89.)

Seeding filters: Adding nitrifying bacteria to a new pond or filter to "kick start" colonies of the bacteria in the pond.

Shadecloth: Woven synthetic material which provides a certain percentage of shade from the sun (from 20% to 100%).

Slime algae: Various forms of algae which cover pond walls, plants and water features. As their name suggests, the algae are soft and slimy making them difficult to remove by hand. (For more information, see *Slime algae* on page 127.)

Soft water: Water which has a pH below 7 (that is, acidic water).

Strain: A strain is a slightly different form of the same species.

Stratified: A pond becomes stratified (layered) when the surface water heats up forming a distinct layer of warm water lying over the denser cold water at the bottom of the pond.

String algae: See *Hair algae* on page 126.

Submergents: Plants that live entirely under the surface of the water.

Submersible: Able to operate underwater.

Sub-phylum: A division of a phylum.

Sump: The lowest area of a pond.

Sump pump: A type of submersible pump designed to pump dirty water (water containing solid particles of matter) from a sump.

Swim bladder: An internal sac in a fish which takes in or expels gases (oxygen etc.) to change the buoyancy of a fish so that it can go up or down in the water without using energy to swim.

Teflon: A type of plastic.

Transformer: An electric device which "transforms" electricity from one voltage to another. With fishpond equipment, the transformers convert electricity to a lower, safer voltage.

***Trichodina*:** A genus of protozoans that live on the skin and gills of fish. Some species are parasitic and they can seriously affect fish health. (For more information, see *Trichodina* in the table on page 88.)

Ultraviolet clarifier / UV clarifier: Also called an ultraviolet filter, it consists of a housing that contains an electric globe which emits ultraviolet light. As water flows through the housing, the light kills microalgae in the water. (For more information, see *UV clarifier* on page 50.)

Velvet disease: This disease gives fish a slimy, dusty look. It is caused by certain single-celled algae species which infect the skin of the fish. (*For more information, see Velvet disease* in the table on page 88.)

Vinyl: A type of plastic.

Vortex filter: *See Centrifuge filter* on page 144.

Water chemistry: All the chemical factors that contribute to the environment in water. For fishponds, the important ones are dissolved oxygen, pH, hardness, salinity, free ammonia, nitrite, nitrate, phosphate, herbicides, pesticides, and heavy metals.

Water Garden: A garden containing ponds and/or water features.

Water feature: Any statue, fountain, waterfall, cascade, and so on placed in a fishpond for artistic effect. (For more information, see *Water features* on page 55.)

Water quality: The physical, chemical and biological characteristics of water. (For more information, see *Water quality standards* on page 140.)

Water exchange: The changing of a percentage of a pond's water on a regular basis to help prevent toxins such as heavy metals from reaching levels that are dangerous to fish. (For more information, see *Keep the pond clean and exchange water* on page 117.)

Waterwall: Any wall down which water flows. (For more information, see *Waterwalls* on page 58.)

Waterwall trough: The water container at the top of a waterwall. Water is pumped to the trough which distributes it so it flows back to the pond as a falling sheet or by trickling down the wall.

White spot (ich): A fish disease caused by protozoan parasites (Scientific name: *Ichthyophthirius multifilis*) which burrow under the skin of fish, giving the fish the appearance of having white spots. (For more information, see *White spot* in the table on page 88.)

Zeolite: A natural clay which adsorbs ammonia from water. (For more information, see *Zeolite* on page 115.)

Printed in Great Britain
by Amazon.co.uk, Ltd.,
Marston Gate.